C-1000 CAREER EXAMINATION SERIES

*This is your
PASSBOOK for...*

Supervisor (Social Work)

*Test Preparation Study Guide
Questions & Answers*

COPYRIGHT NOTICE

This book is SOLELY intended for, is sold ONLY to, and its use is RESTRICTED to individual, bona fide applicants or candidates who qualify by virtue of having seriously filed applications for appropriate license, certificate, professional and/or promotional advancement, higher school matriculation, scholarship, or other legitimate requirements of education and/or governmental authorities.

This book is NOT intended for use, class instruction, tutoring, training, duplication, copying, reprinting, excerption, or adaptation, etc., by:

1) Other publishers
2) Proprietors and/or Instructors of "Coaching" and/or Preparatory Courses
3) Personnel and/or Training Divisions of commercial, industrial, and governmental organizations
4) Schools, colleges, or universities and/or their departments and staffs, including teachers and other personnel
5) Testing Agencies or Bureaus
6) Study groups which seek by the purchase of a single volume to copy and/or duplicate and/or adapt this material for use by the group as a whole without having purchased individual volumes for each of the members of the group
7) Et al.

Such persons would be in violation of appropriate Federal and State statutes.

PROVISION OF LICENSING AGREEMENTS – Recognized educational, commercial, industrial, and governmental institutions and organizations, and others legitimately engaged in educational pursuits, including training, testing, and measurement activities, may address request for a licensing agreement to the copyright owners, who will determine whether, and under what conditions, including fees and charges, the materials in this book may be used them. In other words, a licensing facility exists for the legitimate use of the material in this book on other than an individual basis. However, it is asseverated and affirmed here that the material in this book CANNOT be used without the receipt of the express permission of such a licensing agreement from the Publishers. Inquiries re licensing should be addressed to the company, attention rights and permissions department.

All rights reserved, including the right of reproduction in whole or in part, in any form or by any means, electronic or mechanical, including photocopying, recording, or by any information storage and retrieval system, without permission in writing from the Publisher.

Copyright © 2025 by
National Learning Corporation

212 Michael Drive, Syosset, NY 11791
(516) 921-8888 • www.passbooks.com
E-mail: info@passbooks.com

PASSBOOK® SERIES

THE *PASSBOOK® SERIES* has been created to prepare applicants and candidates for the ultimate academic battlefield – the examination room.

At some time in our lives, each and every one of us may be required to take an examination – for validation, matriculation, admission, qualification, registration, certification, or licensure.

Based on the assumption that every applicant or candidate has met the basic formal educational standards, has taken the required number of courses, and read the necessary texts, the *PASSBOOK® SERIES* furnishes the one special preparation which may assure passing with confidence, instead of failing with insecurity. Examination questions – together with answers – are furnished as the basic vehicle for study so that the mysteries of the examination and its compounding difficulties may be eliminated or diminished by a sure method.

This book is meant to help you pass your examination provided that you qualify and are serious in your objective.

The entire field is reviewed through the huge store of content information which is succinctly presented through a provocative and challenging approach – the question-and-answer method.

A climate of success is established by furnishing the correct answers at the end of each test.

You soon learn to recognize types of questions, forms of questions, and patterns of questioning. You may even begin to anticipate expected outcomes.

You perceive that many questions are repeated or adapted so that you can gain acute insights, which may enable you to score many sure points.

You learn how to confront new questions, or types of questions, and to attack them confidently and work out the correct answers.

You note objectives and emphases, and recognize pitfalls and dangers, so that you may make positive educational adjustments.

Moreover, you are kept fully informed in relation to new concepts, methods, practices, and directions in the field.

You discover that you are actually taking the examination all the time: you are preparing for the examination by "taking" an examination, not by reading extraneous and/or supererogatory textbooks.

In short, this PASSBOOK®, used directedly, should be an important factor in helping you to pass your test.

SUPERVISOR (SOCIAL WORK)

DUTIES
Under supervision, supervises a unit or group of social work, auxiliary, and other personnel engaged in providing social work services; performs related duties as required.

EXAMPLES OF TYPICAL TASKS
Screens cases, makes work assignments, reads, and reviews workers' case records and reports, and evaluates work performance; gives guidance to subordinate staff in social work techniques, methods, and practices; conducts individual and group staff conferences; trains staff in relevant policies and procedures; works cooperatively with physicians, nurses, and other professional personnel; participates in conferences with higher-level supervisory personnel and with representatives of federal, state, city, and voluntary social work agencies, organizations and groups; cooperates with community service agencies to utilize available resources; handles a caseload, including more difficult cases; prepares and supervises the preparation of case records and required reports.

SCOPE OF THE EXAMINATION
The multiple-choice test may include questions on knowledge and interpretation of agency rules, regulations and procedures relative to social work; health and mental health standards, as mandated by regulatory agencies; generic social work principles, practices, and techniques including knowledge of social systems, support services, crisis intervention, psychosocial assessments, and psychiatric evaluations; principles and techniques of supervision, including planning, organizing, delegation, scheduling, and training and staff development; developing and maintaining constructive relationships with staff, patients and their families, public and private agency representatives and hospital personnel of other disciplines, including problem recognition and problem solving; written expression, including maintaining accurate documentation in preparing forms and reports; and other related areas.

HOW TO TAKE A TEST

I. YOU MUST PASS AN EXAMINATION

A. *WHAT EVERY CANDIDATE SHOULD KNOW*

Examination applicants often ask us for help in preparing for the written test. What can I study in advance? What kinds of questions will be asked? How will the test be given? How will the papers be graded?

As an applicant for a civil service examination, you may be wondering about some of these things. Our purpose here is to suggest effective methods of advance study and to describe civil service examinations.

Your chances for success on this examination can be increased if you know how to prepare. Those "pre-examination jitters" can be reduced if you know what to expect. You can even experience an adventure in good citizenship if you know why civil service exams are given.

B. *WHY ARE CIVIL SERVICE EXAMINATIONS GIVEN?*

Civil service examinations are important to you in two ways. As a citizen, you want public jobs filled by employees who know how to do their work. As a job seeker, you want a fair chance to compete for that job on an equal footing with other candidates. The best-known means of accomplishing this two-fold goal is the competitive examination.

Exams are widely publicized throughout the nation. They may be administered for jobs in federal, state, city, municipal, town or village governments or agencies.

Any citizen may apply, with some limitations, such as the age or residence of applicants. Your experience and education may be reviewed to see whether you meet the requirements for the particular examination. When these requirements exist, they are reasonable and applied consistently to all applicants. Thus, a competitive examination may cause you some uneasiness now, but it is your privilege and safeguard.

C. *HOW ARE CIVIL SERVICE EXAMS DEVELOPED?*

Examinations are carefully written by trained technicians who are specialists in the field known as "psychological measurement," in consultation with recognized authorities in the field of work that the test will cover. These experts recommend the subject matter areas or skills to be tested; only those knowledges or skills important to your success on the job are included. The most reliable books and source materials available are used as references. Together, the experts and technicians judge the difficulty level of the questions.

Test technicians know how to phrase questions so that the problem is clearly stated. Their ethics do not permit "trick" or "catch" questions. Questions may have been tried out on sample groups, or subjected to statistical analysis, to determine their usefulness.

Written tests are often used in combination with performance tests, ratings of training and experience, and oral interviews. All of these measures combine to form the best-known means of finding the right person for the right job.

II. HOW TO PASS THE WRITTEN TEST

A. NATURE OF THE EXAMINATION

To prepare intelligently for civil service examinations, you should know how they differ from school examinations you have taken. In school you were assigned certain definite pages to read or subjects to cover. The examination questions were quite detailed and usually emphasized memory. Civil service exams, on the other hand, try to discover your present ability to perform the duties of a position, plus your potentiality to learn these duties. In other words, a civil service exam attempts to predict how successful you will be. Questions cover such a broad area that they cannot be as minute and detailed as school exam questions.

In the public service similar kinds of work, or positions, are grouped together in one "class." This process is known as *position-classification*. All the positions in a class are paid according to the salary range for that class. One class title covers all of these positions, and they are all tested by the same examination.

B. FOUR BASIC STEPS

1) Study the announcement

How, then, can you know what subjects to study? Our best answer is: "Learn as much as possible about the class of positions for which you've applied." The exam will test the knowledge, skills and abilities needed to do the work.

Your most valuable source of information about the position you want is the official exam announcement. This announcement lists the training and experience qualifications. Check these standards and apply only if you come reasonably close to meeting them.

The brief description of the position in the examination announcement offers some clues to the subjects which will be tested. Think about the job itself. Review the duties in your mind. Can you perform them, or are there some in which you are rusty? Fill in the blank spots in your preparation.

Many jurisdictions preview the written test in the exam announcement by including a section called "Knowledge and Abilities Required," "Scope of the Examination," or some similar heading. Here you will find out specifically what fields will be tested.

2) Review your own background

Once you learn in general what the position is all about, and what you need to know to do the work, ask yourself which subjects you already know fairly well and which need improvement. You may wonder whether to concentrate on improving your strong areas or on building some background in your fields of weakness. When the announcement has specified "some knowledge" or "considerable knowledge," or has used adjectives like "beginning principles of…" or "advanced … methods," you can get a clue as to the number and difficulty of questions to be asked in any given field. More questions, and hence broader coverage, would be included for those subjects which are more important in the work. Now weigh your strengths and weaknesses against the job requirements and prepare accordingly.

3) Determine the level of the position

Another way to tell how intensively you should prepare is to understand the level of the job for which you are applying. Is it the entering level? In other words, is this the position in which beginners in a field of work are hired? Or is it an intermediate or advanced level? Sometimes this is indicated by such words as "Junior" or "Senior" in the class title. Other jurisdictions use Roman numerals to designate the level – Clerk I, Clerk II, for example. The word "Supervisor" sometimes appears in the title. If the level is not indicated by the title, check the description of duties. Will you be working under very close supervision, or will you have responsibility for independent decisions in this work?

4) Choose appropriate study materials

Now that you know the subjects to be examined and the relative amount of each subject to be covered, you can choose suitable study materials. For beginning level jobs, or even advanced ones, if you have a pronounced weakness in some aspect of your training, read a modern, standard textbook in that field. Be sure it is up to date and has general coverage. Such books are normally available at your library, and the librarian will be glad to help you locate one. For entry-level positions, questions of appropriate difficulty are chosen – neither highly advanced questions, nor those too simple. Such questions require careful thought but not advanced training.

If the position for which you are applying is technical or advanced, you will read more advanced, specialized material. If you are already familiar with the basic principles of your field, elementary textbooks would waste your time. Concentrate on advanced textbooks and technical periodicals. Think through the concepts and review difficult problems in your field.

These are all general sources. You can get more ideas on your own initiative, following these leads. For example, training manuals and publications of the government agency which employs workers in your field can be useful, particularly for technical and professional positions. A letter or visit to the government department involved may result in more specific study suggestions, and certainly will provide you with a more definite idea of the exact nature of the position you are seeking.

III. KINDS OF TESTS

Tests are used for purposes other than measuring knowledge and ability to perform specified duties. For some positions, it is equally important to test ability to make adjustments to new situations or to profit from training. In others, basic mental abilities not dependent on information are essential. Questions which test these things may not appear as pertinent to the duties of the position as those which test for knowledge and information. Yet they are often highly important parts of a fair examination. For very general questions, it is almost impossible to help you direct your study efforts. What we can do is to point out some of the more common of these general abilities needed in public service positions and describe some typical questions.

1) General information

Broad, general information has been found useful for predicting job success in some kinds of work. This is tested in a variety of ways, from vocabulary lists to questions about current events. Basic background in some field of work, such as sociology or economics, may be sampled in a group of questions. Often these are principles which have become familiar to most persons through exposure rather than through formal training. It is difficult to advise you how to study for these questions; being alert to the world around you is our best suggestion.

2) Verbal ability

An example of an ability needed in many positions is verbal or language ability. Verbal ability is, in brief, the ability to use and understand words. Vocabulary and grammar tests are typical measures of this ability. Reading comprehension or paragraph interpretation questions are common in many kinds of civil service tests. You are given a paragraph of written material and asked to find its central meaning.

3) **Numerical ability**

Number skills can be tested by the familiar arithmetic problem, by checking paired lists of numbers to see which are alike and which are different, or by interpreting charts and graphs. In the latter test, a graph may be printed in the test booklet which you are asked to use as the basis for answering questions.

4) **Observation**

A popular test for law-enforcement positions is the observation test. A picture is shown to you for several minutes, then taken away. Questions about the picture test your ability to observe both details and larger elements.

5) **Following directions**

In many positions in the public service, the employee must be able to carry out written instructions dependably and accurately. You may be given a chart with several columns, each column listing a variety of information. The questions require you to carry out directions involving the information given in the chart.

6) **Skills and aptitudes**

Performance tests effectively measure some manual skills and aptitudes. When the skill is one in which you are trained, such as typing or shorthand, you can practice. These tests are often very much like those given in business school or high school courses. For many of the other skills and aptitudes, however, no short-time preparation can be made. Skills and abilities natural to you or that you have developed throughout your lifetime are being tested.

Many of the general questions just described provide all the data needed to answer the questions and ask you to use your reasoning ability to find the answers. Your best preparation for these tests, as well as for tests of facts and ideas, is to be at your physical and mental best. You, no doubt, have your own methods of getting into an exam-taking mood and keeping "in shape." The next section lists some ideas on this subject.

IV. KINDS OF QUESTIONS

Only rarely is the "essay" question, which you answer in narrative form, used in civil service tests. Civil service tests are usually of the short-answer type. Full instructions for answering these questions will be given to you at the examination. But in case this is your first experience with short-answer questions and separate answer sheets, here is what you need to know:

1) Multiple-choice Questions

Most popular of the short-answer questions is the "multiple choice" or "best answer" question. It can be used, for example, to test for factual knowledge, ability to solve problems or judgment in meeting situations found at work.

A multiple-choice question is normally one of three types—

- It can begin with an incomplete statement followed by several possible endings. You are to find the one ending which *best* completes the statement, although some of the others may not be entirely wrong.
- It can also be a complete statement in the form of a question which is answered by choosing one of the statements listed.

- It can be in the form of a problem – again you select the best answer.

Here is an example of a multiple-choice question with a discussion which should give you some clues as to the method for choosing the right answer:

When an employee has a complaint about his assignment, the action which will *best* help him overcome his difficulty is to
- A. discuss his difficulty with his coworkers
- B. take the problem to the head of the organization
- C. take the problem to the person who gave him the assignment
- D. say nothing to anyone about his complaint

In answering this question, you should study each of the choices to find which is best. Consider choice "A" – Certainly an employee may discuss his complaint with fellow employees, but no change or improvement can result, and the complaint remains unresolved. Choice "B" is a poor choice since the head of the organization probably does not know what assignment you have been given, and taking your problem to him is known as "going over the head" of the supervisor. The supervisor, or person who made the assignment, is the person who can clarify it or correct any injustice. Choice "C" is, therefore, correct. To say nothing, as in choice "D," is unwise. Supervisors have and interest in knowing the problems employees are facing, and the employee is seeking a solution to his problem.

2) True/False Questions

The "true/false" or "right/wrong" form of question is sometimes used. Here a complete statement is given. Your job is to decide whether the statement is right or wrong.

SAMPLE: A roaming cell-phone call to a nearby city costs less than a non-roaming call to a distant city.

This statement is wrong, or false, since roaming calls are more expensive.

This is not a complete list of all possible question forms, although most of the others are variations of these common types. You will always get complete directions for answering questions. Be sure you understand *how* to mark your answers – ask questions until you do.

V. RECORDING YOUR ANSWERS

Computer terminals are used more and more today for many different kinds of exams.

For an examination with very few applicants, you may be told to record your answers in the test booklet itself. Separate answer sheets are much more common. If this separate answer sheet is to be scored by machine – and this is often the case – it is highly important that you mark your answers correctly in order to get credit.

An electronic scoring machine is often used in civil service offices because of the speed with which papers can be scored. Machine-scored answer sheets must be marked with a pencil, which will be given to you. This pencil has a high graphite content which responds to the electronic scoring machine. As a matter of fact, stray dots may register as answers, so do not let your pencil rest on the answer sheet while you are pondering the correct answer. Also, if your pencil lead breaks or is otherwise defective, ask for another.

Since the answer sheet will be dropped in a slot in the scoring machine, be careful not to bend the corners or get the paper crumpled.

The answer sheet normally has five vertical columns of numbers, with 30 numbers to a column. These numbers correspond to the question numbers in your test booklet. After each number, going across the page are four or five pairs of dotted lines. These short dotted lines have small letters or numbers above them. The first two pairs may also have a "T" or "F" above the letters. This indicates that the first two pairs only are to be used if the questions are of the true-false type. If the questions are multiple choice, disregard the "T" and "F" and pay attention only to the small letters or numbers.

Answer your questions in the manner of the sample that follows:

32. The largest city in the United States is
    A. Washington, D.C.
    B. New York City
    C. Chicago
    D. Detroit
    E. San Francisco

1) Choose the answer you think is best. (New York City is the largest, so "B" is correct.)
2) Find the row of dotted lines numbered the same as the question you are answering. (Find row number 32)
3) Find the pair of dotted lines corresponding to the answer. (Find the pair of lines under the mark "B.")
4) Make a solid black mark between the dotted lines.

VI. BEFORE THE TEST

Common sense will help you find procedures to follow to get ready for an examination. Too many of us, however, overlook these sensible measures. Indeed, nervousness and fatigue have been found to be the most serious reasons why applicants fail to do their best on civil service tests. Here is a list of reminders:

- Begin your preparation early – Don't wait until the last minute to go scurrying around for books and materials or to find out what the position is all about.
- Prepare continuously – An hour a night for a week is better than an all-night cram session. This has been definitely established. What is more, a night a week for a month will return better dividends than crowding your study into a shorter period of time.
- Locate the place of the exam – You have been sent a notice telling you when and where to report for the examination. If the location is in a different town or otherwise unfamiliar to you, it would be well to inquire the best route and learn something about the building.
- Relax the night before the test – Allow your mind to rest. Do not study at all that night. Plan some mild recreation or diversion; then go to bed early and get a good night's sleep.
- Get up early enough to make a leisurely trip to the place for the test – This way unforeseen events, traffic snarls, unfamiliar buildings, etc. will not upset you.
- Dress comfortably – A written test is not a fashion show. You will be known by number and not by name, so wear something comfortable.

- Leave excess paraphernalia at home – Shopping bags and odd bundles will get in your way. You need bring only the items mentioned in the official notice you received; usually everything you need is provided. Do not bring reference books to the exam. They will only confuse those last minutes and be taken away from you when in the test room.
- Arrive somewhat ahead of time – If because of transportation schedules you must get there very early, bring a newspaper or magazine to take your mind off yourself while waiting.
- Locate the examination room – When you have found the proper room, you will be directed to the seat or part of the room where you will sit. Sometimes you are given a sheet of instructions to read while you are waiting. Do not fill out any forms until you are told to do so; just read them and be prepared.
- Relax and prepare to listen to the instructions
- If you have any physical problem that may keep you from doing your best, be sure to tell the test administrator. If you are sick or in poor health, you really cannot do your best on the exam. You can come back and take the test some other time.

VII. AT THE TEST

The day of the test is here and you have the test booklet in your hand. The temptation to get going is very strong. Caution! There is more to success than knowing the right answers. You must know how to identify your papers and understand variations in the type of short-answer question used in this particular examination. Follow these suggestions for maximum results from your efforts:

1) Cooperate with the monitor

The test administrator has a duty to create a situation in which you can be as much at ease as possible. He will give instructions, tell you when to begin, check to see that you are marking your answer sheet correctly, and so on. He is not there to guard you, although he will see that your competitors do not take unfair advantage. He wants to help you do your best.

2) Listen to all instructions

Don't jump the gun! Wait until you understand all directions. In most civil service tests you get more time than you need to answer the questions. So don't be in a hurry. Read each word of instructions until you clearly understand the meaning. Study the examples, listen to all announcements and follow directions. Ask questions if you do not understand what to do.

3) Identify your papers

Civil service exams are usually identified by number only. You will be assigned a number; you must not put your name on your test papers. Be sure to copy your number correctly. Since more than one exam may be given, copy your exact examination title.

4) Plan your time

Unless you are told that a test is a "speed" or "rate of work" test, speed itself is usually not important. Time enough to answer all the questions will be provided, but this does not mean that you have all day. An overall time limit has been set. Divide the total time (in minutes) by the number of questions to determine the approximate time you have for each question.

5) Do not linger over difficult questions

If you come across a difficult question, mark it with a paper clip (useful to have along) and come back to it when you have been through the booklet. One caution if you do this – be sure to skip a number on your answer sheet as well. Check often to be sure that you have not lost your place and that you are marking in the row numbered the same as the question you are answering.

6) Read the questions

Be sure you know what the question asks! Many capable people are unsuccessful because they failed to *read* the questions correctly.

7) Answer all questions

Unless you have been instructed that a penalty will be deducted for incorrect answers, it is better to guess than to omit a question.

8) Speed tests

It is often better NOT to guess on speed tests. It has been found that on timed tests people are tempted to spend the last few seconds before time is called in marking answers at random – without even reading them – in the hope of picking up a few extra points. To discourage this practice, the instructions may warn you that your score will be "corrected" for guessing. That is, a penalty will be applied. The incorrect answers will be deducted from the correct ones, or some other penalty formula will be used.

9) Review your answers

If you finish before time is called, go back to the questions you guessed or omitted to give them further thought. Review other answers if you have time.

10) Return your test materials

If you are ready to leave before others have finished or time is called, take ALL your materials to the monitor and leave quietly. Never take any test material with you. The monitor can discover whose papers are not complete, and taking a test booklet may be grounds for disqualification.

VIII. EXAMINATION TECHNIQUES

1) Read the general instructions carefully. These are usually printed on the first page of the exam booklet. As a rule, these instructions refer to the timing of the examination; the fact that you should not start work until the signal and must stop work at a signal, etc. If there are any *special* instructions, such as a choice of questions to be answered, make sure that you note this instruction carefully.

2) When you are ready to start work on the examination, that is as soon as the signal has been given, read the instructions to each question booklet, underline any key words or phrases, such as *least, best, outline, describe* and the like. In this way you will tend to answer as requested rather than discover on reviewing your paper that you *listed without describing*, that you selected the *worst* choice rather than the *best* choice, etc.

3) If the examination is of the objective or multiple-choice type – that is, each question will also give a series of possible answers: A, B, C or D, and you are called upon to select the best answer and write the letter next to that answer on your answer paper – it is advisable to start answering each question in turn. There may be anywhere from 50 to 100 such questions in the three or four hours allotted and you can see how much time would be taken if you read through all the questions before beginning to answer any. Furthermore, if you come across a question or group of questions which you know would be difficult to answer, it would undoubtedly affect your handling of all the other questions.

4) If the examination is of the essay type and contains but a few questions, it is a moot point as to whether you should read all the questions before starting to answer any one. Of course, if you are given a choice – say five out of seven and the like – then it is essential to read all the questions so you can eliminate the two that are most difficult. If, however, you are asked to answer all the questions, there may be danger in trying to answer the easiest one first because you may find that you will spend too much time on it. The best technique is to answer the first question, then proceed to the second, etc.

5) Time your answers. Before the exam begins, write down the time it started, then add the time allowed for the examination and write down the time it must be completed, then divide the time available somewhat as follows:
    - If 3-1/2 hours are allowed, that would be 210 minutes. If you have 80 objective-type questions, that would be an average of 2-1/2 minutes per question. Allow yourself no more than 2 minutes per question, or a total of 160 minutes, which will permit about 50 minutes to review.
    - If for the time allotment of 210 minutes there are 7 essay questions to answer, that would average about 30 minutes a question. Give yourself only 25 minutes per question so that you have about 35 minutes to review.

6) The most important instruction is to *read each question* and make sure you know what is wanted. The second most important instruction is to *time yourself properly* so that you answer every question. The third most important instruction is to *answer every question*. Guess if you have to but include something for each question. Remember that you will receive no credit for a blank and will probably receive some credit if you write something in answer to an essay question. If you guess a letter – say "B" for a multiple-choice question – you may have guessed right. If you leave a blank as an answer to a multiple-choice question, the examiners may respect your feelings but it will not add a point to your score. Some exams may penalize you for wrong answers, so in such cases *only*, you may not want to guess unless you have some basis for your answer.

7) Suggestions
    a. Objective-type questions
        1. Examine the question booklet for proper sequence of pages and questions
        2. Read all instructions carefully
        3. Skip any question which seems too difficult; return to it after all other questions have been answered
        4. Apportion your time properly; do not spend too much time on any single question or group of questions

5. Note and underline key words – *all, most, fewest, least, best, worst, same, opposite,* etc.
6. Pay particular attention to negatives
7. Note unusual option, e.g., unduly long, short, complex, different or similar in content to the body of the question
8. Observe the use of "hedging" words – *probably, may, most likely,* etc.
9. Make sure that your answer is put next to the same number as the question
10. Do not second-guess unless you have good reason to believe the second answer is definitely more correct
11. Cross out original answer if you decide another answer is more accurate; do not erase until you are ready to hand your paper in
12. Answer all questions; guess unless instructed otherwise
13. Leave time for review

b. Essay questions
1. Read each question carefully
2. Determine exactly what is wanted. Underline key words or phrases.
3. Decide on outline or paragraph answer
4. Include many different points and elements unless asked to develop any one or two points or elements
5. Show impartiality by giving pros and cons unless directed to select one side only
6. Make and write down any assumptions you find necessary to answer the questions
7. Watch your English, grammar, punctuation and choice of words
8. Time your answers; don't crowd material

8) Answering the essay question

Most essay questions can be answered by framing the specific response around several key words or ideas. Here are a few such key words or ideas:

M's: manpower, materials, methods, money, management
P's: purpose, program, policy, plan, procedure, practice, problems, pitfalls, personnel, public relations

a. Six basic steps in handling problems:
1. Preliminary plan and background development
2. Collect information, data and facts
3. Analyze and interpret information, data and facts
4. Analyze and develop solutions as well as make recommendations
5. Prepare report and sell recommendations
6. Install recommendations and follow up effectiveness

b. Pitfalls to avoid
1. *Taking things for granted* – A statement of the situation does not necessarily imply that each of the elements is necessarily true; for example, a complaint may be invalid and biased so that all that can be taken for granted is that a complaint has been registered

2. *Considering only one side of a situation* – Wherever possible, indicate several alternatives and then point out the reasons you selected the best one
3. *Failing to indicate follow up* – Whenever your answer indicates action on your part, make certain that you will take proper follow-up action to see how successful your recommendations, procedures or actions turn out to be
4. *Taking too long in answering any single question* – Remember to time your answers properly

IX. AFTER THE TEST

Scoring procedures differ in detail among civil service jurisdictions although the general principles are the same. Whether the papers are hand-scored or graded by machine we have described, they are nearly always graded by number. That is, the person who marks the paper knows only the number – never the name – of the applicant. Not until all the papers have been graded will they be matched with names. If other tests, such as training and experience or oral interview ratings have been given, scores will be combined. Different parts of the examination usually have different weights. For example, the written test might count 60 percent of the final grade, and a rating of training and experience 40 percent. In many jurisdictions, veterans will have a certain number of points added to their grades.

After the final grade has been determined, the names are placed in grade order and an eligible list is established. There are various methods for resolving ties between those who get the same final grade – probably the most common is to place first the name of the person whose application was received first. Job offers are made from the eligible list in the order the names appear on it. You will be notified of your grade and your rank as soon as all these computations have been made. This will be done as rapidly as possible.

People who are found to meet the requirements in the announcement are called "eligibles." Their names are put on a list of eligible candidates. An eligible's chances of getting a job depend on how high he stands on this list and how fast agencies are filling jobs from the list.

When a job is to be filled from a list of eligibles, the agency asks for the names of people on the list of eligibles for that job. When the civil service commission receives this request, it sends to the agency the names of the three people highest on this list. Or, if the job to be filled has specialized requirements, the office sends the agency the names of the top three persons who meet these requirements from the general list.

The appointing officer makes a choice from among the three people whose names were sent to him. If the selected person accepts the appointment, the names of the others are put back on the list to be considered for future openings.

That is the rule in hiring from all kinds of eligible lists, whether they are for typist, carpenter, chemist, or something else. For every vacancy, the appointing officer has his choice of any one of the top three eligibles on the list. This explains why the person whose name is on top of the list sometimes does not get an appointment when some of the persons lower on the list do. If the appointing officer chooses the second or third eligible, the No. 1 eligible does not get a job at once, but stays on the list until he is appointed or the list is terminated.

X. HOW TO PASS THE INTERVIEW TEST

The examination for which you applied requires an oral interview test. You have already taken the written test and you are now being called for the interview test – the final part of the formal examination.

You may think that it is not possible to prepare for an interview test and that there are no procedures to follow during an interview. Our purpose is to point out some things you can do in advance that will help you and some good rules to follow and pitfalls to avoid while you are being interviewed.

What is an interview supposed to test?

The written examination is designed to test the technical knowledge and competence of the candidate; the oral is designed to evaluate intangible qualities, not readily measured otherwise, and to establish a list showing the relative fitness of each candidate – as measured against his competitors – for the position sought. Scoring is not on the basis of "right" and "wrong," but on a sliding scale of values ranging from "not passable" to "outstanding." As a matter of fact, it is possible to achieve a relatively low score without a single "incorrect" answer because of evident weakness in the qualities being measured.

Occasionally, an examination may consist entirely of an oral test – either an individual or a group oral. In such cases, information is sought concerning the technical knowledges and abilities of the candidate, since there has been no written examination for this purpose. More commonly, however, an oral test is used to supplement a written examination.

Who conducts interviews?

The composition of oral boards varies among different jurisdictions. In nearly all, a representative of the personnel department serves as chairman. One of the members of the board may be a representative of the department in which the candidate would work. In some cases, "outside experts" are used, and, frequently, a businessman or some other representative of the general public is asked to serve. Labor and management or other special groups may be represented. The aim is to secure the services of experts in the appropriate field.

However the board is composed, it is a good idea (and not at all improper or unethical) to ascertain in advance of the interview who the members are and what groups they represent. When you are introduced to them, you will have some idea of their backgrounds and interests, and at least you will not stutter and stammer over their names.

What should be done before the interview?

While knowledge about the board members is useful and takes some of the surprise element out of the interview, there is other preparation which is more substantive. It *is* possible to prepare for an oral interview – in several ways:

1) Keep a copy of your application and review it carefully before the interview

This may be the only document before the oral board, and the starting point of the interview. Know what education and experience you have listed there, and the sequence and dates of all of it. Sometimes the board will ask you to review the highlights of your experience for them; you should not have to hem and haw doing it.

2) Study the class specification and the examination announcement

Usually, the oral board has one or both of these to guide them. The qualities, characteristics or knowledges required by the position sought are stated in these documents. They offer valuable clues as to the nature of the oral interview. For example, if the job involves supervisory responsibilities, the announcement will usually indicate that knowledge of modern supervisory methods and the qualifications of the candidate as a supervisor will be tested. If so, you can expect such questions, frequently in the form of a hypothetical situation which you are expected to solve. NEVER go into an oral without knowledge of the duties and responsibilities of the job you seek.

3) Think through each qualification required

Try to visualize the kind of questions you would ask if you were a board member. How well could you answer them? Try especially to appraise your own knowledge and background in each area, *measured against the job sought*, and identify any areas in which you are weak. Be critical and realistic – do not flatter yourself.

4) Do some general reading in areas in which you feel you may be weak

For example, if the job involves supervision and your past experience has NOT, some general reading in supervisory methods and practices, particularly in the field of human relations, might be useful. Do NOT study agency procedures or detailed manuals. The oral board will be testing your understanding and capacity, not your memory.

5) Get a good night's sleep and watch your general health and mental attitude

You will want a clear head at the interview. Take care of a cold or any other minor ailment, and of course, no hangovers.

What should be done on the day of the interview?

Now comes the day of the interview itself. Give yourself plenty of time to get there. Plan to arrive somewhat ahead of the scheduled time, particularly if your appointment is in the fore part of the day. If a previous candidate fails to appear, the board might be ready for you a bit early. By early afternoon an oral board is almost invariably behind schedule if there are many candidates, and you may have to wait. Take along a book or magazine to read, or your application to review, but leave any extraneous material in the waiting room when you go in for your interview. In any event, relax and compose yourself.

The matter of dress is important. The board is forming impressions about you – from your experience, your manners, your attitude, and your appearance. Give your personal appearance careful attention. Dress your best, but not your flashiest. Choose conservative, appropriate clothing, and be sure it is immaculate. This is a business interview, and your appearance should indicate that you regard it as such. Besides, being well groomed and properly dressed will help boost your confidence.

Sooner or later, someone will call your name and escort you into the interview room. *This is it.* From here on you are on your own. It is too late for any more preparation. But remember, you asked for this opportunity to prove your fitness, and you are here because your request was granted.

What happens when you go in?

The usual sequence of events will be as follows: The clerk (who is often the board stenographer) will introduce you to the chairman of the oral board, who will introduce you to the other members of the board. Acknowledge the introductions before you sit down. Do not be surprised if you find a microphone facing you or a stenotypist sitting by. Oral interviews are usually recorded in the event of an appeal or other review.

Usually the chairman of the board will open the interview by reviewing the highlights of your education and work experience from your application – primarily for the benefit of the other members of the board, as well as to get the material into the record. Do not interrupt or comment unless there is an error or significant misinterpretation; if that is the case, do not hesitate. But do not quibble about insignificant matters. Also, he will usually ask you some question about your education, experience or your present job – partly to get you to start talking and to establish the interviewing "rapport." He may start the actual questioning, or turn it over to one of the other members. Frequently, each member undertakes the questioning on a particular area, one in which he is perhaps most competent, so you can expect each member to participate in the examination. Because time is limited, you may also expect some rather abrupt switches in the direction the questioning takes, so do not be upset by it. Normally, a board member will not pursue a single line of questioning unless he discovers a particular strength or weakness.

After each member has participated, the chairman will usually ask whether any member has any further questions, then will ask you if you have anything you wish to add. Unless you are expecting this question, it may floor you. Worse, it may start you off on an extended, extemporaneous speech. The board is not usually seeking more information. The question is principally to offer you a last opportunity to present further qualifications or to indicate that you have nothing to add. So, if you feel that a significant qualification or characteristic has been overlooked, it is proper to point it out in a sentence or so. Do not compliment the board on the thoroughness of their examination – they have been sketchy, and you know it. If you wish, merely say, "No thank you, I have nothing further to add." This is a point where you can "talk yourself out" of a good impression or fail to present an important bit of information. Remember, *you close the interview yourself.*

The chairman will then say, "That is all, Mr. _____, thank you." Do not be startled; the interview is over, and quicker than you think. Thank him, gather your belongings and take your leave. Save your sigh of relief for the other side of the door.

How to put your best foot forward

Throughout this entire process, you may feel that the board individually and collectively is trying to pierce your defenses, seek out your hidden weaknesses and embarrass and confuse you. Actually, this is not true. They are obliged to make an appraisal of your qualifications for the job you are seeking, and they want to see you in your best light. Remember, they must interview all candidates and a non-cooperative candidate may become a failure in spite of their best efforts to bring out his qualifications. Here are 15 suggestions that will help you:

1) Be natural – Keep your attitude confident, not cocky

If you are not confident that you can do the job, do not expect the board to be. Do not apologize for your weaknesses, try to bring out your strong points. The board is interested in a positive, not negative, presentation. Cockiness will antagonize any board member and make him wonder if you are covering up a weakness by a false show of strength.

2) Get comfortable, but don't lounge or sprawl

Sit erectly but not stiffly. A careless posture may lead the board to conclude that you are careless in other things, or at least that you are not impressed by the importance of the occasion. Either conclusion is natural, even if incorrect. Do not fuss with your clothing, a pencil or an ashtray. Your hands may occasionally be useful to emphasize a point; do not let them become a point of distraction.

3) Do not wisecrack or make small talk

This is a serious situation, and your attitude should show that you consider it as such. Further, the time of the board is limited – they do not want to waste it, and neither should you.

4) Do not exaggerate your experience or abilities

In the first place, from information in the application or other interviews and sources, the board may know more about you than you think. Secondly, you probably will not get away with it. An experienced board is rather adept at spotting such a situation, so do not take the chance.

5) If you know a board member, do not make a point of it, yet do not hide it

Certainly you are not fooling him, and probably not the other members of the board. Do not try to take advantage of your acquaintanceship – it will probably do you little good.

6) Do not dominate the interview

Let the board do that. They will give you the clues – do not assume that you have to do all the talking. Realize that the board has a number of questions to ask you, and do not try to take up all the interview time by showing off your extensive knowledge of the answer to the first one.

7) Be attentive

You only have 20 minutes or so, and you should keep your attention at its sharpest throughout. When a member is addressing a problem or question to you, give him your undivided attention. Address your reply principally to him, but do not exclude the other board members.

8) Do not interrupt

A board member may be stating a problem for you to analyze. He will ask you a question when the time comes. Let him state the problem, and wait for the question.

9) Make sure you understand the question

Do not try to answer until you are sure what the question is. If it is not clear, restate it in your own words or ask the board member to clarify it for you. However, do not haggle about minor elements.

10) Reply promptly but not hastily

A common entry on oral board rating sheets is "candidate responded readily," or "candidate hesitated in replies." Respond as promptly and quickly as you can, but do not jump to a hasty, ill-considered answer.

11) Do not be peremptory in your answers

A brief answer is proper – but do not fire your answer back. That is a losing game from your point of view. The board member can probably ask questions much faster than you can answer them.

12) Do not try to create the answer you think the board member wants

He is interested in what kind of mind you have and how it works – not in playing games. Furthermore, he can usually spot this practice and will actually grade you down on it.

13) Do not switch sides in your reply merely to agree with a board member

Frequently, a member will take a contrary position merely to draw you out and to see if you are willing and able to defend your point of view. Do not start a debate, yet do not surrender a good position. If a position is worth taking, it is worth defending.

14) Do not be afraid to admit an error in judgment if you are shown to be wrong

The board knows that you are forced to reply without any opportunity for careful consideration. Your answer may be demonstrably wrong. If so, admit it and get on with the interview.

15) Do not dwell at length on your present job

The opening question may relate to your present assignment. Answer the question but do not go into an extended discussion. You are being examined for a *new* job, not your present one. As a matter of fact, try to phrase ALL your answers in terms of the job for which you are being examined.

Basis of Rating

Probably you will forget most of these "do's" and "don'ts" when you walk into the oral interview room. Even remembering them all will not ensure you a passing grade. Perhaps you did not have the qualifications in the first place. But remembering them will help you to put your best foot forward, without treading on the toes of the board members.

Rumor and popular opinion to the contrary notwithstanding, an oral board wants you to make the best appearance possible. They know you are under pressure – but they also want to see how you respond to it as a guide to what your reaction would be under the pressures of the job you seek. They will be influenced by the degree of poise you display, the personal traits you show and the manner in which you respond.

ABOUT THIS BOOK

This book contains tests divided into Examination Sections. Go through each test, answering every question in the margin. We have also attached a sample answer sheet at the back of the book that can be removed and used. At the end of each test look at the answer key and check your answers. On the ones you got wrong, look at the right answer choice and learn. Do not fill in the answers first. Do not memorize the questions and answers, but understand the answer and principles involved. On your test, the questions will likely be different from the samples. Questions are changed and new ones added. If you understand these past questions you should have success with any changes that arise. Tests may consist of several types of questions. We have additional books on each subject should more study be advisable or necessary for you. Finally, the more you study, the better prepared you will be. This book is intended to be the last thing you study before you walk into the examination room. Prior study of relevant texts is also recommended. NLC publishes some of these in our Fundamental Series. Knowledge and good sense are important factors in passing your exam. Good luck also helps. So now study this Passbook, absorb the material contained within and take that knowledge into the examination. Then do your best to pass that exam.

EXAMINATION SECTION

EXAMINATION SECTION
TEST 1

DIRECTIONS: Each question or incomplete statement is followed by several suggested answers or completions. Select the one that BEST answers the question or completes the statement. *PRINT THE LETTER OF THE CORRECT ANSWER IN THE SPACE AT THE RIGHT.*

1. For children, divorce has been identified as a risk factor for
    I. being abused
    II. substance abuse
    III. lower academic achievement
    IV. criminal involvement

    A. I and II
    B. II and III
    C. II, III and IV
    D. I, II, III and IV

    1.____

2. In formulating useful goals with clients, a social worker is guided by several principles. Which of the following is NOT one of these principles?

    A. Goal formulation is often delimited by the purpose of the agency, and may necessitate referral.
    B. It is necessary to designate a target person whose condition is to be changed or maintained.
    C. Goals should always be stated positively in terms of *doing* something, rather than simply *not doing* something.
    D. The establishment of a time frame for achievement is counterproductive in the formulation of goals.

    2.____

3. In selecting members for group social work, homogeneity will prove most important regarding

    A. intelligence
    B. ethnicity
    C. age, especially for young children
    D. common interests

    3.____

4. A practitioner will probably NOT work well with diverse populations if he

    A. believes he is free from any racist attitudes, beliefs, or feelings
    B. is comfortable with the differences between himself and clients
    C. is flexible in applying theories to specific situations
    D. is open to being challenged and teste

    4.____

5. "Non-verbal" messages of practitioners and clients refer to

    A. statements that nobody should be permitted to make in an interpersonal relationship
    B. ideas and thoughts that are left unrevealed

    5.____

1

C. written or otherwise documented statements about problems, recommendations, and solutions
D. the entire range of facial and body expressions that communicate feelings

6. During an assessment interview, a social worker should usually avoid asking _____ questions.

   A. "why"
   B. probing
   C. open-ended
   D. closed-ended

6._____

7. Common goals of foster parent organizations include each of the following, EXCEPT

   A. elevating the public's regard for foster care
   B. the facilitation of adoption by foster parents
   C. influencing legislation that concerns children and natural parents
   D. disseminating information among foster parents

7._____

8. "Homeostasis" is a concept that has been traditionally used to describe how

   A. organisms maintain a constant external environment
   B. organisms keep themselves stable through self-regulating mechanisms
   C. humans tend to form groups or tribes around food supplies
   D. humans display a broad but fixed range of behaviors

8._____

9. A practitioner welcomes a client at the door of his office by saying, "Come in and sit down." He gestures to the room and the chair inside. This gesture is a _____ of the practitioner's verbal message

   A. complementation
   B. repetition
   C. regulation
   D. contradiction

9._____

10. In interviewing clients, practitioners should be careful to avoid nonverbal behaviors that are generally considered to be negative. These gestures include each of the following, EXCEPT

    A. body rotated slightly away from the client
    B. crossing and recrossing legs
    C. slightly backward body lean
    D. frequent eye contact

10._____

11. A practitioner asks himself: "Is our agency's program doing what it had hoped to do?" He is asking himself a _____ question.

    A. client outcome assessment
    B. intervention effectiveness
    C. process evaluation
    D. program evaluation

11._____

12. Of the following, which provides the BEST definition of the process of social work?

12._____

A. A distinct set of skills that allow the worker to tap into a variety of skills to improve conditions surrounding the client system
B. A helping activity undertaken to improve social functioning through direct involvement with the client or the systems that impact him
C. A series of programmed interventions designed to shape the client and his environment
D. A professional service to people in need who are unwilling or unable to act in their own best interests

13. Which of the following is NOT a basic component of social work "competence," as defined by the NASW?

    A. Accepting responsibility or employment only on the basis of existing competence or the intention to acquire the necessary competence.
    B. Not allowing their personal problems, psychosocial distress, legal problems, substance abuse, or mental health difficulties to interfere with professional judgment and performance.
    C. Basing practice on recognized knowledge, including empirically based knowledge, relevant to social work and social work ethics.
    D. Striving to become and remain proficient in professional practice and the performance of professional functions.

14. For practitioners who hope to draw upon Piaget's theory of cognitive development in their work with clients, probably the biggest shortcoming of his theory is that it

    A. does not examine any cognitive development beyond adolescence
    B. pigeonholes clients into distinct categories
    C. excludes questions of morality
    D. does not examine behavioral components of cognitions

15. Which of the following is true of institutional discrimination?

    A. It is often concealed through legal maneuverings.
    B. It is limited to large, formal organizations.
    C. It is woven into the fabric of society.
    D. It is a construction of the elite.

16. In the solution-focused model of intervention, the best way to solve problems is to

    A. discover when the client is not having a problem, and then build on that
    B. understand the goals and ambitions of the client
    C. determine the function that the problematic behavior serves for the client
    D. define the problem in terms of the client's external environment

17. A child in Piaget's preoperational stage
    I. is capable of altruism
    II. uses transductive reasoning
    III. is egocentric
    IV. derives thought from sensation and movement

    A. I and II
    B. I, III and IV

C. II and III
D. I, II, III and IV

18. Which of the following is NOT a primary human motive? 18.____

    A. Desire for competence
    B. Avoidance of pain
    C. Thirst
    D. Hunger

19. Summarizing clients' statements is an active listening strategy that is often useful for distilling statements into their important elements. The FIRST step in developing a good summarization of client statements during an interview is to 19.____

    A. covertly restating the message or series of messages to yourself
    B. listening for the presence of "feeling" words
    C. ask the client to summarize for herself
    D. identify any relevant patterns themes, or multiple elements

20. Each of the following is considered to be a desirable outcome of an initial interview with an applicant for social services, EXCEPT that the applicant 20.____

    A. leaves confident of working with the practitioner or case manager toward a satisfactory solution
    B. understands his/her responsibilities in the treatment or intervention
    C. feels free to express him/herself
    D. feeling some rapport with the practitioner or case manager

21. When counseling clients, social work practitioners will generally be effective if they 21.____
    I. are able to recognize and accept their own power
    II. can focus on the present moment
    III. remain in the active process of developing their own counseling style
    IV. are not afraid to offer advice

    A. I and III
    B. I, II and III
    C. II, III and IV
    D. I, II, III and IV

22. According to the NASW's code of ethics, social workers who have direct knowledge of a social work colleague's incompetence should FIRST 22.____

    A. consult with that colleague when feasible and assist the colleague in taking remedial action
    B. take action through the appropriate channels established by the employers or agency
    C. notify the NASW and any appropriate licensing and regulating bodies
    D. solicit the opinion of at least one other social worker with approximately equal qualifications and responsibilities to determine a course of action

23. Countertransference, if recognized by the practitioner, can be a useful element in a client relationship. Often, however, it is not helpful or even hurtful. Hurtful forms typically involve each of the following, EXCEPT countertransference that 23.____

A. causes a practitioner to emit subtle clues that "lead" the client
B. causes a practitioner to adopt the role the client wants us to play in his or her traditional "script"
C. is used at a distance to generate empathy for the client
D. blinds a practitioner from an important area of exploration

24. During any intervention, a social worker's final activities are aimed at _____ in the client's everyday functioning.

    I. stabilizing success
    II. generalizing outcomes
    III. preventing recidivism
    IV. restricting options

A. I and II
B. I and III
C. II, III and IV
D. I, II, III and IV

25. In the documentation and report writing phase of assessment, a service coordinator's documentation responsibilities usually consist of

A. social histories and intake summaries
B. medical and social histories
C. staff notes and mental status examinations
D. intake summaries and staff notes

26. A social work practitioner is MOST likely to increase the chances of his clients' connecting with the appropriate services when he

A. refers clients to other more skilled professionals in the hope that these professionals will be able to determine how best to meet the clients' needs
B. promotes self determination by providing a list of agencies in the area and allowing the clients to decide who can best meet their needs
C. acquire expertise in as many areas of social work practice as possible, in order to directly provide needed services
D. becomes knowledgeable about programs and providers available, and actively brokers needed services

27. One explanation for the steady increase in the divorce rate in the United States is that industrialization and urbanization led to a change in the roles played by family members. This explanation is consistent with the _____ perspective.

A. symbolic interaction
B. structural functionalist
C. subcultural
D. social conflict

28. One of the most significant criticisms about the use of strategic planning in human services organizations is that it

A. leaves many stakeholders in the dark about the organization's objectives
B. limits responsiveness to changing community needs

C. erodes employee morale and commitment to the organizational mission
D. is often too abstract to be useful in day-to-day management

29. The way in which a practitioner conceptualizes a client's problem configuration is known as

    A. conceptualization
    B. the internal working model
    C. mental set
    D. framing

30. Significant factors that have contributed to the changing nature of American families since the 1970s include
    I. an increase in births outside marriage
    II. a greater number of remarriages in which partners bring children from previous relationships
    III. altered gender role expectations
    IV. an increase in the number of partners who divorce or separate

    A. I, II and IV
    B. I and III
    C. III only
    D. I, II, III and IV

31. Culture maintains boundaries in each of the following ways, EXCEPT by

    A. instilling a sense of genuineness about the alternatives peculiar to a society
    B. constructing symbols and meanings
    C. limiting the ranges of acceptable behavior and attitudes
    D. establishing the tendency for people to think of other societies as inferior

32. The solution-focused perspective defines a client who describes a problem but isn't willing to work on solving it as a

    A. resistor
    B. complainant
    C. dam-builder
    D. procrastinator

33. During an assessment interview, a practitioner is trying to identify the range of problems that a client is experiencing. Which of the following communication skills is most appropriately used for this purpose?

    A. Open-ended questions
    B. Closed-ended questions
    C. Confrontation
    D. Interpretation

34. Social workers who have unresolved personal conflicts should

    A. recognize that their problems may interfere with the effectiveness and avoid activities or responses that could harm a client
    B. repress any anxiety-provoking issues in their own lives before attempting to work with others

C. use their experience to lead clients in a mutual resolution of these problems
D. resolve these conflicts before planning a client intervention and ideally, before meeting the client at all.

35. Based largely on the understanding that all people break rules at one time or another, _____ theorists make the assumption that what we call "deviant" is actually part of an overall pattern of normality.   35._____

    A. labeling
    B. social Darwinism
    C. conflict
    D. order

36. Rural clients tend to evaluate social workers on the basis of   36._____

    A. the level of education the worker has achieved
    B. help delivered or problems solved
    C. the type of intervention used
    D. areas of specialization

37. A client is having trouble at work. He tells the practitioner "I have a hard time relating to authority figures." He is describing his problem behavior   37._____

    A. in a way that places responsibility squarely on himself
    B. covertly
    C. in nonbehavioral terms
    D. without any affective cues

38. The practice of limiting a client's right to self-determination in order to protect him or her from self-harm is known in social work as   38._____

    A. gatekeeping
    B. paternalism
    C. delimiting behavior
    D. proxy

39. Which of the following is LEAST likely to be a symptom of stress?   39._____

    A. Emotional instability
    B. Lethargy
    C. Sleep problems
    D. Digestive problems

40. In the traditional clinical model of school social work, a practitioner was probably LEAST likely to execute the role of   40._____

    A. enabler
    B. consultant
    C. supporter
    D. advocate

41. When advocating for a client, the first attempt at advocacy should always be

    A. a legal challenge
    B. a formal appeal
    C. temperate persuasion
    D. widely spread publicity about the client's case

42. During regular meetings with his practitioner, a client has the tendency to ascribe the achievements of others to good luck or easy tasks, while assuming his failures to be due to a lack of ability or experience. The client's thinking is a phenomenon known as

    A. fundamental attribution bias
    B. the Hawthorne effect
    C. self-serving bias
    D. the halo effect

43. The responsibilities of social work intern instructors typically include each of the following, EXCEPT

    A. clearly stating roles and responsibilities of interns in the field
    B. clearly stating the roles and responsibilities of site supervisors
    C. acting on site supervisors' recommendations following a negative intern evaluation
    D. developing clear field placement policies

44. A teenage client has been having problems in school he is constantly being disciplined for being disruptive. Discussions with the client reveal that even though he has lost several privileges at school, he is reluctant to give up his disruptive behavior because of the attention it brings in from his peers. The attention of the client's peers is an example of a(n)

    A. secondary gain
    B. behavioral consequence
    C. negative reinforcement
    D. cognitive dissonance

45. Which of the following is NOT a typical purpose of client self-monitoring?

    A. To shift the burden of decision-making onto the client
    B. To validate the accuracy of the client's reports during interviews
    C. To test out hunches about the problem.
    D. To help practitioner and client gain information about what actually occurs with respect to the problem in real-life situations

46. Which of the following is a "lower-order" human need, as identified in Maslow's hierarchy?

    A. Belonging
    B. Status
    C. Fulfillment
    D. Security

47. Gene, a social worker, finds himself wanting to solve his client's problems with alcohol dependency, which are similar to problems Gene's own son went through several years ago. Gene gives advice and is frustrated when the client doesn't follow through on his suggestions. Gene's emotional reactions to his client are based on

    A. countertransference
    B. nurturing
    C. transference
    D. empathy

48. In the termination phase of treatment, strategies for maintaining client gains may include each of the following, EXCEPT

    A. increasing the client's sense of mastery through realistic praise
    B. anticipating and planning for possible future difficulties
    C. highlighting and specifying the client's role in maintaining change
    D. teaching the client to deal with problems that underlie a coping pattern

49. After receiving a notification about a 10-year-old boy's underperfor-mance at school, a social worker has tried twice to arrange a meeting with the boy's 28-year-old mother, who works long hours as a waitress and has sole responsibility for his care. Both times, the mother has cancelled the meeting at the last minute, citing sudden work conflicts.
    The social worker schedules an in-home visit to the boy's family but when he arrives, he is told by the boy that the mother is at work. The child's grandmother also lives in the home, but is bedridden, and the boy and his sister help care for her. The family's apartment is in disarray, with dirty dishes stacked in the sink and on the stovetop. Laundry is strewn about in wrinkled piles. The social worker observes no alcohol in the house, and the grandmother, who is cooperative, says that her daughter doesn't drink, and never has.
    As the social worker continues to monitor this family, he should be especially alert for signs of

    A. a personality disorder on the part of the mother
    B. child abuse
    C. substance abuse
    D. child neglect

50. Within practice settings that call upon the practitioner's knowledge and skill at all levels of the organization, the social work profession is considered to be a(n) _____ discipline.

    A. primary
    B. secondary
    C. collegial
    D. ancillary

51. Among gays and lesbians, stress and a lack of emotional support have been shown to contribute to

    A. high rates of alcoholism
    B. promiscuity
    C. identity fragmentation
    D. erratic employment patterns

52. An elderly client is particularly concerned about being "bothered" all the time by a social work practitioner who frequently visits her home. To avoid too much discomfort on the part of the client, the practitioner has the client sign several blank consent forms so that her medical history can be sent to several agencies that might offer supportive services. In this case, the worker has

    A. violated the principle of informed consent
    B. hit upon a key strategy for avoiding burnout
    C. demonstrated ignorance of the eligibility rules for most service agencies
    D. found an ethical strategy for streamlining an often frustrating bureaucracy

53. The most common diagnoses for people who complete suicide are

    A. schizophrenia and substance abuse
    B. depressive illness and borderline personality disorder
    C. depressive illness and alcoholism
    D. schizophrenia and chronic metabolic disease

54. The mother of a 14-year-old girl telephoned crisis services, telling the worker that her son had just locked and barricaded himself in his room. Earlier, she had overheard a conversation between the boy and his girlfriend that was clearly a fight. She is concerned because the boy had tried to overdose after the end of an earlier relationship.
    A worker was immediately dispatched to the residence. After a lengthy conversation in which the worker successfully established rapport with the boy, the boy agreed to let the worker in.
    Thus far, crisis services and the worker have followed the formula of Roberts' Seven-Stage Crisis Intervention Model. As a next step, the worker will attempt to

    A. explore alternatives to suicide, such as inpatient or outpatient services
    B. identify and validate the boy's emotions
    C. develop an action plan with the boy
    D. have the boy identify what he views as the major problem or problems

55. The primary goal of crisis intervention can best be described as

    A. protecting the client from a situation in which he or she has become more likely to experience a traumatic event than other people
    B. helping the client to identify and endure the long-term consequences of a traumatic event
    C. protecting a client from self-harm following a traumatic event
    D. helping the client to identify and cope with the sense of "disequilibrium" in the aftermath of a trauma

56. A practitioner discovers that a client is behaving in a way that is seriously damaging both to himself and a close relative. While respecting the concept of self-determination and confidentiality, the practitioner should

    A. warn the client that he (the practitioner) has an obligation to divulge the client's behavior to the appropriate agency or authority, and then do so
    B. attempt to dissuade the client from further engaging in behavior that is harmful
    C. immediately alert the authorities
    D. refer the client to a social services worker who has more experience in this specific type of behavior

57. In order to serve effectively in rural communities, social work practitioners would most likely need to incorporate the concepts of _____ into their practice.

    A. nature and seasonal fluctuation
    B. self-reliance and mutual aid
    C. land and ownership
    D. religion and spirituality

58. Which of the following is NOT typically included in a service agreement between a practitioner and a client?

    A. Description of the agency's programs and services
    B. Fees for service or arrangements for reimbursement
    C. Theoretical framework for the relationship
    D. Time frames for the provision of services

59. From a legal perspective, case records

    A. belong to the practitioner who created them
    B. belong to the client
    C. belong to the agency at which they are physically held
    D. are for the benefit of the client

60. A practitioner is speaking to a client via cellular phone. The practitioner should be aware that
    I. there is a chance that the call could be intercepted by an unauthorized party
    II. the client may not be in a private place
    III. telephone conversations are not considered to be a public service
    IV. complete privacy cannot be assured

    A. I and II
    B. I, II, and IV
    C. III only
    D. I, II, III and IV

61. The basic assumptions underlying social work administration do NOT include the statement that

    A. each person who works within the agency should be considered a stakeholder in agency outcomes
    B. administration is largely the process of securing and transforming community resources
    C. the major contributions toward the improvement of administration come from management itself
    D. the agency has the primary responsibility for the creation and control of its own destiny

62. Most Asian Americans who are seeking from a social work practitioner are looking for a professional who is

    A. nondirective
    B. problem-focused
    C. goal-oriented
    D. experiential in focus

63. Privileged communication is NOT

    A. widely varying in state-to-state legal definitions
    B. usually waived if a third party is present
    C. particularly difficult to protect when working with married couples
    D. protected no matter what the risks involved

64. In devising a treatment plan, a practitioner begins with client tasks that can be managed fairly easily and with some success, before moving on to the larger issues that are causing problems. In doing so, the practitioner is adhering to the rule of

    A. successive approximations
    B. object orientation
    C. positive reinforcement
    D. mental set

65. "Preparatory empathy" is a process that is used by a practitioner in order to

    A. insure against client deception
    B. streamline an intervention by figuring some things out in advance
    C. choose necessary resources or services
    D. make him more aware of issues or barriers that might be encountered

66. The federal WIC program specifically targets the health and welfare of

    A. abused children
    B. adoptive families
    C. pregnant women and newborn children
    D. unskilled laborers who have been injured on the job

67. Of all Hispanics living the United States, those of Mexican descent account for about _____ percent of the total.

    A. 20
    B. 40
    C. 60
    D. 80

68. From her first few meetings with a client, a social work practitioner has begun to form an impression. If the practitioner seeks out additional information that will help to confirm or deny her existing impressions, she will be engaging in

    A. cognitive integration
    B. active perception
    C. offensive perception
    D. thematic apperception

69. A social worker is using the person-in-environment (PIE) system of client assessment. In describing the environmental problems that affect a client's social functioning, the social worker will rely on six groupings of social system problems. Which of the following is NOT one of the groupings used in the PIE system?

    A. Economic/basic need
    B. Judicial/legal system

C. Physical health
D. Education and training

70. Basic social work values that influence professional practice include each of the following, EXCEPT

   A. self-determination
   B. the inherent uniqueness of a person
   C. individualism
   D. the inherent worth and dignity of a person

71. Which step in the listening process involves the assignment of meaning to a message?

   A. Encoding
   B. Attending
   C. Understanding
   D. Selecting

72. Qualitative social work research

   A. observes people in natural settings and focuses on the meaning they assign to experiences.
   B. is analyzed through the use of bivariate methods
   C. details the past in order to understand present conditions
   D. compares statistics from number of cases

73. When a worker attempts to "cement" a referral, she is attempting to

   A. make sure the client is connected to the suggested resource
   B. make the working relationship into a strong enough bond that the client will be sure to follow through
   C. use software or another evaluative tool that confirms the appropriateness of the client to the proposed resource
   D. suggest to the client in advance that the referral will result in success

74. In working with a client, a practitioner is careful to avoid singling out one or two obvious client characteristics as the reason for everything the person does. The tendency to do this is known as

   A. stereotyping
   B. scripting
   C. over-attribution
   D. highballing

75. A group's sense of ethnic identity is affected by the
    I. degree to which the members' physical appearances differ from those in mainstream society
    II. size of the group
    III. amount of power the group has
    IV. extent of assimilation

    A. I only
    B. I and III
    C. II and IV
    D. I, II, III and IV

75.____

KEY (CORRECT ANSWERS)

1. D	16. A	31. A	46. D	61. C
2. D	17. C	32. B	47. A	62. A
3. C	18. A	33. A	48. D	63. D
4. A	19. A	34. A	49. D	64. A
5. D	20. B	35. A	50. A	65. D
6. A	21. B	36. B	51. A	66. C
7. B	22. A	37. C	52. A	67. C
8. B	23. C	38. B	53. C	68. B
9. B	24. A	39. B	54. D	69. C
10. D	25. D	40. D	55. D	70. C
11. D	26. D	41. C	56. A	71. C
12. B	27. B	42. A	57. B	72. A
13. A	28. D	43. C	58. C	73. A
14. A	29. A	44. A	59. B	74. C
15. C	30. D	45. A	60. B	75. D

TEST 2

DIRECTIONS: Each question or incomplete statement is followed by several suggested answers or completions. Select the one that BEST answers the question or completes the statement. *PRINT THE LETTER OF THE CORRECT ANSWER IN THE SPACE AT THE RIGHT.*

1. In the _____ style of conflict management, the parties attempt to separate themselves from the problem.

    A. cooperative
    B. nonconfrontational
    C. mediative
    D. settlement

    1.____

2. The purposes of staff notes, or progress notes, include
    I. recording client's responses to services
    II. connecting a service to a key issue
    III. describing client status
    IV. providing direction for ongoing treatment

    A. I only
    B. I, II and III
    C. III and IV
    D. I, II, III and IV

    2.____

3. A genogram is an assessment tool that

    A. involves DNA sampling
    B. defers consideration of current family relationships
    C. gives a picture of family relationships over at least three generations
    D. uses statistical measures to calculate the probability of an intervention's success

    3.____

4. Which of the following is NOT a belief of stage theorists?

    A. The progression of stages is biologically programmed.
    B. Children pass through the same stages in the same sequence.
    C. Stages are usually marked by age ranges.
    D. As children progress through the stages, the differences between them are quantitative.

    4.____

5. During the opening phase of a client interview, the practitioner should probably spend most of his time and thoughts on

    A. self-disclosure
    B. negotiating a working contract
    C. interpreting behaviors
    D. explaining agency rules and protocols

    5.____

6. Behaviors commonly associated with substance abuse include
    I. a withdrawal from responsibility
    II. unusual outbreaks of temper
    III. abrupt changes in quality or output of work
    IV. wearing sunglasses at inappropriate times

    6.____

A. I and II
B. I, II and III
C. II and IV
D. I, II, III and IV

7. Which of the following would a practitioner typically do FIRST in a problem assessment interview?

    A. Identify client coping skills
    B. Identify the range of client problems
    C. Prioritize and select issues and problems for discussion
    D. Identify consequences of problem behaviors

8. A social worker's primary ethical duty is to

    A. effect social justice
    B. promote the welfare of the client
    C. respect diversity
    D. avoid dependent relationships

9. The person-centered model of human behavior views the major reason for maladjustment as a(n)

    A. failure to set a self-actualizing tendency in motion
    B. inability to establish unconditional positive regard
    C. incongruence between self-concept and experience
    D. unresolved childhood frustrations

10. The person-in-environment (PIE) system of client assessment is a four-factor system. Factor _____ provides a statement of the client's physical health problems.

    A. I
    B. II
    C. III
    D. IV

11. An adolescent client tells her social worker that she feels she is the only person in the world who has ever had such strong unrequited love for another person—the boy who sits next to her in geometry class. The component of adolescent egocentrism being enacted by the girl is the

    A. all-or-none fallacy
    B. imaginary audience
    C. questionable cause
    D. personal fable

12. Research into interpersonal relationships suggests that women often build relationships through shared positive feelings, while men often build relationships through

    A. shared activities
    B. shared opinions
    C. metacommunication
    D. impression management

13. Which of the following is NOT typically a purpose of assessment?

    A. To identify the controlling or contributing variables associated with a client's problem
    B. To launch the first phase of treatment
    C. To educate and motivate the client by sharing views about the problem
    D. To plan effective interventions and strategies

14. Persuading clients to abandon mistaken ways of thinking is a goal of

    A. client-centered therapy
    B. operant conditioning
    C. cognitive therapy
    D. systematic desensitization

15. A practitioner is creating an action plan with an adult client who has decided to leave his current job. Typically, planning such a move requires practitioner and client to move on to

    A. ensure that the work to be done fits an accepted model of treatment
    B. breaking large goals into component parts
    C. making the client aware of the full range of consequences
    D. ensure that this decision meets with the approval of the people who will be affected by it

16. Some of the information in an applicant's file comes from secondary sources. Which of the following is NOT considered a secondary source?

    A. Applicant's family
    B. Referring agency
    C. School
    D. Current staff notes

17. Self-disclosure is considered a "discretionary" response in discussions with clients, because it

    A. is not considered to be therapeutic
    B. is only used if the client requests it
    C. should be used carefully to avoid taking the focus off the client
    D. requires a familiarity with the client's worldview before it is used

18. For a practitioner working from the family systems theory, symptoms of maladjustment in families are usually masked by

    A. the involvement and recommendations of professionals who were previously involved
    B. the presenting crisis or problem that initially brought the family into contact with the agency
    C. abusive relationships
    D. environmental components in the family's community

19. A school social worker is told that one of the kindergartners is running around, out of control, and disrupting the others at naptime. As she attempts to understand the problem, her FIRST step should be to

A. arrange an interview with the school psychologist
B. look into finding an alternative school placement
C. systematically observe the child in the classroom to see how it is managed
D. contact the parents to inform them of the child's behavior problems

20. What is the collective term applied to communication variables such as voice level, pitch, rate, and fluency of speech?

    A. Kinesics
    B. Paralinguistics
    C. Nonverbal messages
    D. Proxemics

21. Although the terms *counseling* and *interviewing* are sometimes used interchangeably in social work, there are differences that should be noted. Which of the following is NOT one of these differences.

    A. Interviewing is a responsibility that can be assumed by most practitioners or case managers.
    B. Interviewing is a more basic process for information gathering and problem solving.
    C. Counseling is a more intensive and personal process.
    D. Counseling is often associated with nonprofessional workers, whereas therapy used to indicate professional interventions.

22. A social worker in the _____ role is conducting "macro" practice.
    I. manager
    II. planner
    III. case manager
    IV. mediator

    A. I and II
    B. I, II and IV
    C. III only
    D. I, II, III and IV

23. The final stage of Elisabeth Kubler-Ross's theory of how people handle the knowledge of their impending death is known as

    A. denial
    B. bargaining
    C. anger
    D. acceptance

24. Probably the most important factor in establishing a working alliance with a client is the

    A. client's belief about whether the practitioner attends and understands
    B. accuracy of the practitioner's assessment of the presenting problem(s)
    C. practitioner's effort to be empathetic
    D. client's initial willingness to change

25. During the assessment phase, the practice of _____ means that the practitioner and client are setting specific objectives.

    A. activating resources
    B. framing solutions
    C. defining the problem
    D. weighing alternatives

26. Reflecting and paraphrasing are two active listening strategies often used by practitioners to help clients become more aware of the implications of their own statements. Basically the difference between reflecting and paraphrasing involves the difference between the

    A. client's words and the client's actions
    B. the emotional (affective) and factual (cognitive) content of messages
    C. way the client perceives the world and the way the world actually is
    D. way the client is expressing a message and the way it is being received by the practitioner

27. The process by which people shape social life by adapting to, negotiating with, and changing social structures is known as

    A. determinism
    B. positivism
    C. human agency
    D. ideology

28. Child welfare is a social work practice area that

    A. focuses on issues, problems, and policies related to the well-being of children
    B. administers school lunches and other benefit programs for low-income children
    C. focuses on increasing the educational potential of children
    D. mainly works to broker adoptions

29. The relationship between social work supervisors and supervisees, which parallels the relationship between social worker and client, has been described in terms of basic relational elements. Which of the following is NOT one of these?

    A. Caring
    B. Rapport
    C. Authority
    D. Trust

30. The _____ model attributes the essential characteristics of consensus, cohesion, stability, reciprocity, and cooperation to society.

    A. evolutionary
    B. conflict
    C. order
    D. symbolic interaction

31. Upholding rules, regulations and restrictions of a social services agency which are not always best for the client is a function of the social worker's role known as

    A. gatekeeping
    B. spoilage
    C. advocacy
    D. bureaucratic blindness

32. A social worker and her client have developed a long-range goal. Now they are determining individual steps that will lead to the achievement of that goal. This is a process known as

    A. chunking
    B. prioritizing
    C. partializing
    D. contracting

33. Community surveys, policy analyses, and case histories are examples of

    A. social studies
    B. ecomaps
    C. needs assessments
    D. genograms

34. In a social services agency that serves teenage runaways, an example of a direct service strategy would be

    A. organizing
    B. counseling
    C. gathering information
    D. planning

35. Compared to others in society, those with superior _____ are more likely to support the status quo.

    A. educational achievement
    B. social locations
    C. value systems
    D. incomes

36. "Primary prevention" means

    A. the severity and duration of a disease or disorder have been reduced
    B. clinical means have been used to provide treatment, such as crisis intervention
    C. a disease or disorder is stopped at its source, and the cause is eliminated
    D. the spread of a disease or disorder among people has been limited

37. Under normal circumstances it is considered acceptable practice for a social worker to disclose a client's confidential information to
    I. the practitioner's supervisor as it relates to the supervisory relationship
    II. professionals who are consulted about assessments or interventions
    III. third-party payers for the purpose of justifying treatment decisions
    IV. close family members for the purpose of developing understanding of the client's particular difficulties

A. I only
B. I and II
C. I, II and III
D. I, II, III and IV

38. A client's feelings of powerlessness can be reduced when a social worker adopts each of the following roles, EXCEPT the role of

   A. resource consultant, who connects the client to goods and services
   B. advocate, who acts as the client's protector in social living matters
   C. sensitizer, who helps the client gain knowledge needed to solve problems
   D. educator, who facilitates the learning and skill development needed for goal setting and task completion

39. The _____ model of human services organization management places the greatest value on maximizing the productivity of the organization.

   A. internal process
   B. open-system
   C. rational goal
   D. human relations

40. During an interview, practitioner and client establish a goal for the client to use her time more efficiently at work and at home. This is an example of a _____ goal.

   A. process
   B. survival
   C. treatment
   D. service

41. One reason people often confuse race and ethnicity is because they

   A. are suspicious of people who are different from themselves
   B. are unaware that race is cultural and ethnicity is biological
   C. see cultural differences and define race in specific, often inaccurate ways
   D. have met few people outside their own race

42. Dual relationships between a practitioner and a client, according to the NASW:

   A. should not be formed if there is any possibility for exploitation or potential harm to the client
   B. are usually an unavoidable part of professional practice
   C. are generally acceptable if social workers take steps to protect clients
   D. are generally acceptable if social workers are careful to avoid legal problems that could damage the status of the social work profession

43. In a family intervention that implements the structural model, the family will be expected to

   A. submit to the direction of the practitioner
   B. solve their own problems
   C. shift their internal alliances
   D. shift blame to the external environment

44. In diversion programs, social workers typically provide

    A. case management services with probation officers in an attempt to prevent recidivism
    B. consultation services about early-release programs for juvenile offenders
    C. counseling services through a network of lay professionals
    D. crisis intervention or referral services aimed at avoiding imprisonment

45. In hospital social work, an example of macropractice would be

    A. connecting with community providers to maintain understanding of community needs
    B. increasing health provider awareness of clients' home environment
    C. engaging clients in planning for their immediate future after discharge
    D. educating clients and families about the implications of a particular illness or disorder

46. A client tells a practitioner that he is distraught over the end of his marriage and wishes he could "just go to sleep forever, be at peace, and not have to feel this pain any more." The practitioner should

    A. assess whether the client is suicidal and intervene if necessary
    B. recognize that such statements are often merely a "cry for help" and urge the client to focus on more practical issues
    C. contact the client's wife and determine whether there is a chance to reconcile
    D. immediately commit the client to a psychiatric facility

47. The presenting problems of most African American clients are rooted in

    A. genetics
    B. personality deficits
    C. stress from external systems
    D. unresolved family conflicts

48. A solution-focused intervention would most likely involve the goal of

    A. a first-order change in the client system
    B. behavioral continuity
    C. a perceptual shift from talking about problems to talking about how to solve them
    D. determining exactly how a problem came into being

49. During an interview in which a client is being evaluated, the client should understand that the

    A. information gained during the interview may be the basis of a report on the client
    B. questions will not be upsetting to him/her
    C. interview will focus on the client's well-being
    D. he or she has implicitly entered into a service contract

50. The _____ theory of rural social work asserts that there are distinct differences between rural and urban areas, and that the urban end of the continuum is associated with social pathology.

A. classical
B. subcultural
C. compositional
D. determinist

51. During the supervisory discussion of a client case, the FIRST topic of discussion should typically be

    A. client dynamics and problems
    B. alternative intervention strategies
    C. a tentative assessment or diagnosis
    D. selection of a general treatment approach

52. The millions of Asian Americans living in the United States today represent a generally _____ population.

    A. prosperous
    B. culturally homogeneous
    C. mainstreamed
    D. heterogeneous

53. Most legal issues encountered by social work practitioners involve

    A. complaints of improper conduct
    B. being sued for negligence or malpractice
    C. being prosecuted for crimes
    D. acting as witnesses in litigation

54. The initial recommended response to a client who is suicidal is

    A. hospitalization and observation
    B. identifying the client's level of seriousness
    C. problem-solving training
    D. crisis intervention and a functional assessment of the suicidal behavior

55. The most common client reactions to the termination of direct social service include each of the following, EXCEPT

    A. pride
    B. ambivalence
    C. satisfaction
    D. denial

56. Most referrals to human service professionals are made by

    A. school systems
    B. health care workers
    C. the courts
    D. word of mouth from friends or family members

57. The term "handicap" refers to a(n)

    A. obstruction that prevents an interface between a disability and the environment
    B. an impairment that limits one's daily activities

C. inability to perform tasks at a level that is generally considered to be socially acceptable
D. loss of use or function of an organ or bodily system

58. When writing case notes, practitioners should always
    I. keep in mind that others may read the notes
    II. compose them immediately after a client meeting
    III. provide as much detail as possible
    IV. use shorthand

    A. I and II
    B. II only
    C. I, II and III
    D. I, II, III and

59. The most frequent cause of child death is

    A. physical abuse
    B. suicide
    C. being left unsupervised or alone for long periods of time
    D. automobile accidents

60. Clients of social service agencies often disagree with either agency policies or a practitioner's actions, or both. If a client demands to know why a particular action was taken and perhaps reverse it, he or she is exercising a right to

    A. confidentiality
    B. due process
    C. privileged information
    D. informed consent

61. Content theories of human motivation argue that

    A. most people dislike change
    B. external consequences determine behavior
    C. most people are affiliation-oriented
    D. internal needs lead to behavior

62. Once a client's service needs are clear, a social worker often helps the client choose the most appropriate service and negotiates the terms of service delivery. Here, the social worker is acting in the role of

    A. broker
    B. consultant
    C. advocate
    D. coordinator

63. When social work practitioners commit errors in working with gay, lesbian, and bisexual clients, these errors most often stem from the

    A. workers' own unconscious prejudices
    B. failure to recognize clients as homosexual, due to a lack of identifying characteristics
    C. identification of client problems as being caused by their sexuality

D. assumption that client problems are unrelated to social oppression or stigma

64. If included statistically as a form of elder abuse, self-neglect would represent about _____ percent of cases reported to state adult protective services agencies.

    A. 5-10
    B. 20-35
    C. 40-50
    D. 60-75

65. Many social workers, especially those who work in institutional settings, use the brief treatment model in their interventions. Which of the following is NOT one of the core assumptions of this model?

    A. Problems are a normal part of life and not a sign of pathology.
    B. Practitioners believe people can change, and communicate this to their clients.
    C. The purpose of treatment is to develop insight into the underlying causes of problems.
    D. Treatment makes use of what the client brings to it

66. Stan, a Native American college student, is seeking information about work programs in the urban community where he lives. When Stan asks a female practitioner at the local agency about it, the practitioner notices that he makes very little eye contact. The practitioner should recognize that Stan

    A. would be more likely to look into her eyes if she were a male
    B. is not likely to follow through with the practitioner's recommendations or referrals
    C. is likely to view direct eye contact as a lack of respect
    D. does not express much faith in the practitioner's abilities

67. The tendency of people to perceive what they expect to perceive is a phenomenon known as

    A. self-serving bias
    B. perceptual set
    C. filtration
    D. fundamental attribution bias

68. A person's satisfaction with communication is based upon a theoretical "sum total" of the positive and negative elements in a message. This sum is a phenomenon known as message

    A. validity
    B. salience
    C. solidity
    D. valence

69. Data about how long or how often a problem occurs before an intervention are known as _____ data.

    A. raw
    B. norming
    C. baseline
    D. skewed

70. In _____ social work, assessment is also known as functional analysis.

   A. narrative
   B. behavioral
   C. feminist
   D. cognitive

71. During an assessment interview, a practitioner asks a client: "How do you feel about the fact that your drinking has harmed your relationship with your daughter?" The practitioner is trying to identify _____ consequences of the client's problem.

   A. contextual
   B. affective
   C. behavioral
   D. somatic

72. For social work research to have a meaningful function, it must be applied by practitioners. One of the major reasons practitioners fail to apply the results of research is that

   A. there is no standard methodology that would make results universally applicable
   B. many studies lack relevance to day-to-day practice decisions
   C. there is still widespread theoretical bias in the design of many studies
   D. most practitioners don't conduct research themselves

73. Of the following social sciences, social work draws most of its professional expertise from

   A. psychology
   B. economics
   C. sociology
   D. anthropology

74. In her meetings with a client, a practitioner has begun to form the perception that he may be using a combination of alcohol and illegal drugs. She decides, during subsequent meetings, to engage in "direct perception checking" in order to confirm or deny this perception. This will involve

   A. paying careful attention to the client's tone of voice
   B. observing the client's behaviors to discover cues that will either confirm or deny her impressions
   C. asking the client if he has a drug or drinking problem
   D. listening more intently to the client's words and language

75. Though practitioner self-disclosure can be a useful tool for helping clients, it is most helpful when its use is carefully assessed beforehand. Generally, practitioners should AVOID making self-disclosure statements

   A. as concise as possible
   B. as a way of introducing oneself to the client
   C. in a way that will regulate the role distance between practitioner and client
   D. similar in content and mood to the client's messages

KEY (CORRECT ANSWERS)

1. A	16. D	31. A	46. A	61. D
2. D	17. C	32. C	47. C	62. A
3. C	18. B	33. A	48. C	63. B
4. D	19. C	34. B	49. A	64. C
5. B	20. B	35. B	50. A	65. C
6. D	21. D	36. C	51. A	66. C
7. C	22. A	37. B	52. D	67. B
8. B	23. D	38. B	53. D	68. D
9. C	24. A	39. C	54. D	69. C
10. D	25. B	40. C	55. D	70. B
11. D	26. B	41. C	56. D	71. B
12. A	27. C	42. A	57. A	72. B
13. B	28. A	43. B	58. C	73. A
14. C	29. C	44. D	59. C	74. B
15. B	30. C	45. A	60. B	75. B

EXAMINATION SECTION
TEST 1

DIRECTIONS: Each question or incomplete statement is followed by several suggested answers or completions. Select the one the BEST answers the question or completes the statement. *PRINT THE LETTER OF THE CORRECT ANSWER IN THE SPACE AT THE RIGHT.*

1. The primary sources of data in most assessments are

    A. completed assessment forms
    B. the client's verbal statements
    C. psychological test results
    D. collateral sources

2. A social worker is fulfilling the role of a "mediator" when he or she

    A. calls attention to the probable social consequences to a new housing development
    B. refers a jobless person to an unemployment agency
    C. evaluates the outcome of a colleague's practice
    D. helps a frustrated wife to clarify her position to a husband

3. In the systems model of human behavior, "division of labor" is an example of

    A. autopoiesis
    B. social control
    C. differentiation
    D. hierarchy

4. After several weeks of behavioral intervention, a child is consistently performing the desired behavior targeted by his parents and a social worker: that is, he is going to bed at the correct time without argument or delaying tactics. Now that he's reached this stage, the social worker recommends that the parents gradually withdraw the prompts and reinforcements that induced the behavior to begin with. This is an example of

    A. extinction
    B. shaping
    C. fading
    D. modeling

5. When working with a group, a social worker encourages decision-making by consensus. Drawbacks to the use of consensus include

    A. involvement of few available group resources
    B. alienation of the minority
    C. time- and energy-intensiveness
    D. decreased likelihood of handling future controversies

6. The primary rationale for the use of a social history for client assessment is that

    A. past behavior is the best predictor of future behavior
    B. the best source of information about a client's situation is the client her/himself
    C. the best protection against legal liability is an exhaustive data set

29

D. problems exist because of an unbalanced reaction between a client system and the environment

7. Most professional codes of ethics provide that a social worker's primary ethical duty is to

   A. respect client privacy and confidentiality
   B. challenge social injustice
   C. work in the best interest of clients
   D. avoid situations that involve ethical conflicts

8. In agency planning, which of the following visual aids will be MOST useful in helping to examine the benefits and drawbacks of different alternative choices

   A. Task planning sheet
   B. Gantt chart
   C. Decision tree
   D. PERT chart

9. Which of the following questions or statements is MOST appropriate for a practitioner in initiating an interview?

   A. "I understand you have a problem."
   B. "You came in here to see me about _____."
   C. "How can I help you today?"
   D. "I'm glad you came in to see me

10. What is the term commonly used to describe children who suffer physical, mental, or emotional injuries inflicted by caretaking adults?

    A. Developmentally disabled
    B. Victims
    C. At risk
    D. Abused or neglected

11. Typically, the questioning process in a social work interview should progress

    A. chronologically
    B. from general to specific
    C. from specific to general
    D. in a series of grouped topical units

12. Assessment is a process that is considered to be the task of the

    A. agency psychiatrist or clinician
    B. social worker
    C. client
    D. social worker and client together

13. A social worker who wants to use a small group as a resource for clients should remember the general rule that the addition of new members, especially resistant ones, should be avoided during the _____ stage of group development.

    A. differentiation
    B. intimacy

C. preaffiliation
D. power and control

14. During an assessment interview with a male high school student, it becomes clear to the practitioner that the boy's behavior problems are related in some way to his frustration at the different expectations of his teachers and his peers concerning the role of a student. The boy is experiencing

    A. inter-role conflict
    B. role ambiguity
    C. intra-role conflict
    D. role incapacity

15. When considering the use of informal resources for an intervention, the social worker should

    A. view informal resources as an inexpensive alternative to formal services
    B. whenever possible, try to "professionalize" or train informal resources to lend them authority
    C. already have some knowledge of available self-help groups in the community
    D. whenever informal resources are identified, try to steer clients toward the ones that are probably most useful

16. Probably the biggest difference between the supervisory role in social work and that of other professions is the

    A. amount of psychological support that must be provided to supervisees
    B. degree of direct involvement in the work of supervisees
    C. predominant use of "soft' criteria in performance evaluations
    D. greater difficulty in matching workers to tasks

17. A social worker is interviewing a woman in a mental hospital who appears lucid but is suspected of having some mental illness. When gathering information, the worker should

    A. explain fully the reason for the interview and ask the client to give her opinion of her mental status
    B. ask short, closed-ended assessment questions up front
    C. administer a standardized assessment that may be evaluated by a psychologist
    D. work assessment questions into the ordinary flow of the conversation

18. A social worker becomes aware of a colleague's incompetent or unethical practice. According to the NASW code, the worker's FIRST obligation is to

    A. inform all of the colleague's relevant clients of the situation
    B. approach the colleague to discuss his/her incapacitation, incompetence, etc.
    C. file a complaint with the NASW
    D. file a complaint with the appropriate licensing board

19. A "communication loop" is completed when

    A. the person to whom the message is addressed begins to respond
    B. the person who initiates the message has completed the transmission
    C. the person to whom the message is addressed receives the message
    D. the person to whom the message is addressed decodes the message

20. Because many parents believe in and utilize corporal punishment as discipline, a social worker must be able to differentiate physical abuse from ordinary spanking or corporal punishment. Which of the following is NOT a useful means of making this distinction?

    A. Parent striking the child in places that are easily injured
    B. Repeated episodes of corporal punishment
    C. Child's report that punishments are severe and painful
    D. Injury to child's body tissue

21. A social worker makes an initial in-home visit to a married couple who have willingly submitted to an intervention regarding their marital problems. During the interview the couple points out that they will be leaving the area in a few weeks, because the wife has been transferred by her employer to a new location. Probably the MOST appropriate plan for dealing with this couple would involve the _____ model of social work.

    A. person-centered
    B. cognitive-behavioral
    C. solution-focused
    D. task-centered

22. The primary purpose of evaluative research in social work is to

    A. measure a client's self-satisfaction
    B. determine whether outcomes can be attributed to an intervention
    C. express the effectiveness of interventions in material terms
    D. determine whether an outcome was achieved

23. Each of the following should be used as a guideline in child placement decisions, EXCEPT

    A. efforts to protect the child should involve as little disruption as possible
    B. use of placement to compel a parent to take some action
    C. involvement of parents and child in the placement decision
    D. maintenance of child's cultural beliefs in placement

24. Which of the following is NOT a factor involved in the decoding of a message?

    A. Relationship with interviewer
    B. Social, emotional, and cognitive barriers
    C. Ethics
    D. Context of interview

25. A practitioner wants to make the parents of an adolescent aware of the behavioral manifestations of depression. Which of the following is LEAST likely to be an indicator?

    A. Sudden tearful reactions
    B. Excessive pleasure-seeking
    C. Decline in school achievement
    D. Jokes about death or dying

26. Which of the following is LEAST likely to be an area of conflict between social workers and attorneys

A. Confidentiality
B. Recording information
C. The best interests of a client
D. The definition of "client"

27. Which of the following typically occurs in the first stage of group therapy?

    A. The members are hostile toward the leader.
    B. Cliques form within the group.
    C. The members talk through the leader and seem to ignore one another.
    D. The members interact with each other tend to ignore the leader.

28. In conducting employee evaluations, a social work supervisor should use _____ as available criteria.
    I. pre-established objective measures such as timeliness
    II. "soft" criteria such as attitude
    III. the supervisor's own work experience
    IV. the performance of others in similar assignments

    A. I only
    B. I and II
    C. I and III
    D. I, II, III and IV

29. Which of the following is NOT a term that is interchangeable with "stepfamily"?

    A. Remarried family
    B. Blended family
    C. Reconstituted family
    D. Renested family

30. A worker refers a client to a colleague who specializes and is trained in law, even though the client requested the service from the worker. Which of the following professional values or ethics is the worker implementing?

    A. Self-determination
    B. Privacy
    C. Competence
    D. Confidentiality

31. Social work practice that is based on behavioral theory assumes that behaviors are determined by

    A. emotions
    B. consequences
    C. values
    D. internal thought processes

32. Which of the following is NOT a symptom associated with bipolar disorder?

    A. Increase in goal-oriented activity
    B. Distractibility
    C. Significant weight loss
    D. Decreased need for sleep

33. A 'helping relationship" between the social worker and client is BEST described as

   A. the goal of any initial contact between worker and client
   B. the medium offered to people in trouble through which they are presented with opportunities
   C. the means by which a worker gains the client's trust to solve problems
   D. a lifeline that is thrown to people in trouble in order to help them out of current problems

34. Communities often contain individuals who are categorized as "AFDC mothers" or "hardcore unemployed" or "AIDS patients," among others. This is a destructive application of the concept of

   A. service delivery
   B. niche
   C. differentiation
   D. diversity

35. The first step in any single-system practice evaluation is to

   A. record baseline data
   B. select suitable measures
   C. implement the intervention
   D. specify the goal

36. A social worker plans a behavioral intervention for a developmentally disabled adult who does not look people in the eye when speaking with them.
Each of the following behavioral strategies may be useful to the intervention, EXCEPT

   A. overcorrection
   B. instruction
   C. prompting
   D. shaping

37. During several in-home visits with a family, the mother repeatedly refuses to acknowledge that her alcoholism is having an adverse effect on others in the household. The MOST appropriate next step for the social worker would be to initiate

   A. a challenge
   B. behavioral rehearsal
   C. self-talk management
   D. a behavioral contract

38. Working-class or low-income marriages are typically characterized by

   A. marriage late in life
   B. flexible divisions of labor
   C. troubled mother-child relationships
   D. emotional distance between partners

39. A researcher repeatedly measures the dependent variable throughout two baseline and two treatment phases of a study to assess whether variability in the dependent variable is due to the influence of the independent variable. She is using a(n) _____ design of measurement.

A. AB
B. ABAB
C. multiple baseline
D. Solomon four-group

40. What is the typical time-frame for crisis intervention?

    A. One to two weeks
    B. Six to eight weeks
    C. At least eight weeks
    D. Six months or more, depending on the nature of the crisis

41. Stigma, once it has become part of a culture, has certain predictable consequences. Which of the following is NOT one of these consequences?

    A. Discrimination
    B. Absorption
    C. Altered self-concept
    D. Development of subculture

42. A social worker is engaged in a one-on-one interview with a 10-year-old boy, in order to investigate allegations of a father's sexual abuse. The allegations were initially brought by the mother, now divorced from the father, and were later corroborated by the boy. The mother and father are engaged in a custody battle for the boy. The boy's account of events is extremely consistent over time, listing the same major events in sequence, but his affect is flathe relates his accounts of abuse in an oddly detached manner. The BEST action for the social worker at this point would be to

    A. terminate the interview and begin criminal proceedings against the father
    B. terminate the interview and refer the child for an immediate psychiatric consultation
    C. ask the mother to join in the interview and see if her account matches the boy's
    D. ask the boy to go into greater detail about the related events, out of sequence, and then repeat the request at a later time

43. When working with individuals or families of native American cultures, it is best to begin by

    A. gathering a social history
    B. using indirect approaches such as analogy or metaphor
    C. asking for open-ended descriptions of family roles
    D. direct questioning

44. In cases of elder abuse, the government may intervene if
    I. the older person requests it
    II. the older person is found at a hearing to be incompetent
    III. the abuse or neglect presents an unacceptable level of danger to the older person
    IV. the abuse is properly reported and recorded by a visiting social services worker

    A. I only
    B. I and II

C. I, II and III
D. I, II, III and IV

45. Which of the following is a guideline that should be observed in developing an assessment questionnaire for clients?

   A. Develop several focused questionnaires rather than a single all-purpose one.
   B. The most sensitive or probing questions should appear near the middle of the questionnaire.
   C. For complex ideas, form two-part questions.
   D. Include only open-ended questions.

46. During the assessment phase of an interview, checklists are most useful for identifying and selecting

   A. problems for intervention
   B. specific objectives
   C. available resources
   D. general goals

47. Which of the following is an advantage associated with the family life-cycle model?

   A. It highlights the special challenges of blended families.
   B. It identifies developmental tasks for families at specific stages.
   C. It is especially applicable to families in minority groups.
   D. It applies to those who do not have children.

48. Before making the decision to advocate on behalf of a client, it is important to consider several factors. Which of the following is NOT one of these?

   A. Client's consent for advocacy.
   B. Whether advocating is the most useful process that can be applied to the situation.
   C. Whether the complaint or decision involves a legitimate grievance
   D. Client's knowledge and feeling about human services.

49. Which of the following is an advantage associated with the use of genograms in client assessment?

   A. Targeting and identification of relevant social supports.
   B. Execution and interpretation require no instruction.
   C. Placement of an individual or family within a social context.
   D. A considerable shortening of the case record.

50. Activities involved in social casework typically include

   A. counseling those with a terminal illness
   B. supervising juvenile probation clients
   C. providing job training
   D. preparing court reports

51. In middle childhood, school-age children are generally concerned with

   A. "good" behavior in order to receive approval from others
   B. behaving appropriately because they fear punishment

C. the concordance of behaviors with an adopted moral code
D. conforming with group standards in order to be rewarded

52. When a social worker/client relationship is characterized by ineffectiveness, the most common reason is that

    A. resources are not available to meet the client's needs
    B. the client has not sufficiently specified his or her needs
    C. an incorrect solution has been identified by the worker
    D. the worker is attempting to keep the relationship on a pleasant level

53. A social history report includes the statement: "The subject claims to have completed high school." This should be included under the heading:

    A. Family Background and Situation
    B. Intellectual functioning
    C. Impressions and Assessment
    D. Such a statement shouldn't appear at all in a social history report.

54. According to Erickson, which of the following stages of psychosocial development occurs FIRST in the human life span?

    A. Initiative vs. guilt
    B. Trust vs. mistrust
    C. Identity vs. role confusion
    D. Autonomy vs. shame and doubt

55. The strategy of "reframing" is most useful for

    A. desensitizing clients to past trauma
    B. classifying client/family problems according to standard diagnostic categories
    C. helping clients to model their own behavior after others'
    D. revealing a client's strengths and opportunities for helping

56. In general, it is believed that interviewers who spend less than a minimum of _____ of an interview listening to the client are more active than they should be.

    A. one-fourth
    B. one-third
    C. one-half
    D. two thirds

57. In the _____ model of social work, the goal of the social worker is to enhance and restore the psychosocial functioning of persons, or to change noxious social conditions that impede the mutually beneficial interaction between person and their environment.

    A. structural-functional
    B. ecological
    C. medical
    D. strategic

58. In social work, "micro" practice usually focuses on

   A. resolving the problems of individuals, families, or small groups
   B. planning, administration, evaluation, and community organizing
   C. developmental activities in the social environment
   D. facilitating communication, mediation, and negotiation

59. _____ theory may prove most productive for the social work practitioner in understanding families of homosexuals, because it introduces unambiguous distinctions between stigma and homosexual behaviors and feelings.

   A. Structural
   B. Object relations
   C. Strategic
   D. Labeling

60. A client tells a practitioner that his main goal for intervention is to decide on a college major. To BEST help this client, the practitioner will assume the role of

   A. enabler
   B. mediator
   C. initiator
   D. educator

61. Which of the following is NOT a guideline for interacting with clients from a Latino culture?

   A. Efforts to foster independence and self-reliance may be interpreted by many Latinos as a lack of concern for others.
   B. Efforts to deal one-on-one with an adolescent client may serve to alienate the parents, especially the mother.
   C. A nonverbal gesture such as lowering the eyes is interpreted by many Latinos as a sign of respect and deference to authority.
   D. In much of Latino culture, the locus of control for problems tends to be much more external than internal.

62. The broadest, most general type of plan used in social work administration is the

   A. plan for meeting objectives
   B. statement of goals
   C. statement of mission
   D. guiding policies

63. In composing a social network grid with a client, which of the following steps is typically performed FIRST?

   A. Dividing acquaintances according to direction of help
   B. Dividing acquaintances according to duration of acquaintance
   C. Identifying people who can help the client in concrete ways
   D. Identifying areas of life in which people impact the client

64. An administrator notices, in several trips through the agency grounds, that a handful of the organization's support staff are often engaged in socializing or other nonproductive activities. The groups are always small and never made up of the same people, and nearly all members of the support staff have received satisfactory evaluations from their supervisor. The socializing does not occur around clients or visiting professionals. Over the past several years, the agency's efficiency record has remained about the same. The agency would probably be BEST served by the view that

    A. rigid controls should be implemented to reduce this behavior
    B. a memorandum should be circulated citing this behavior as a poor example
    C. the behavior may help to relieve boredom and should be ignored
    D. the supervisor should add an item or two to the evaluation that will address this behavior

65. Each of the following is a stage of the dying process described by Kübler-Ross, EXCEPT

    A. acknowledgement
    B. depression
    C. anger
    D. acceptance

66. For a prison inmate, "notice of rights" means the inmate
    I. receives advance notice of what conduct will result in discipline or punishment
    II. receives written notice of any charges against him
    III. is entitled to organize a group meeting for political purposes

    A. I and II
    B. I and III
    C. II and III
    D. I, II and III

67. Which of the following values is NOT generally indigenous to families of Asian heritage?

    A. Inconspicuousness
    B. Perfectionism
    C. Fatalism
    D. Shame as a behavioral influence

68. Most professionals recommend that in order to accurately evaluate the effect of an intervention, baseline data should be collected for no fewer than _____ data points.

    A. 2
    B. 3
    C. 4
    D. 5

69. During an assessment interview, a social worker and a client try to clarify and analyze the client's sense of self. If the worker wants to discover something about the client's self-acceptance, which of the following questions is MOST appropriate?

    A. To what extent do you worry about illness and physical incapacity?
    B. Is what you expect to happen mostly good or mostly bad?

C. Do you enjoy the times when you are alone?
D. Where do your other family members live?

70. Which of the following cognitive traits explains the mistaken belief held by many adolescents that they are invincible or protected from harmful consequences of their behavior?

    A. The personal fable
    B. Object delusion
    C. Egocentrism
    D. Pseudohypocrisy

71. An 18-year-old woman comes to see a social worker at a crisis center one day after being raped on a date. In the interview with this client, the social worker should FIRST:

    A. emphasize medical and legal procedures
    B. obtain factual information about the rape
    C. listen to the client and support her emotionally
    D. help the client establish contact with significant others

72. During a client assessment, each of the following should be considered a useful question, EXCEPT

    A. Can you tell me about times when you've successfully handled a problem like this in the past?
    B. When family members complain about your behavior, what to they say?
    C. How have you managed to cope up to this point?
    D. What do your friends and family seem to like most about you?

73. Norms are MOST accurately described as

    A. attitudes toward life events and processes
    B. assumptions about the world
    C. expectations of the self and others
    D. ideas about what is proper and desirable behavior

74. Generally, when a homeless person or group is removed from a condemned or abandoned property under the law, the most significant legal question to arise is whether

    A. the last owner of the property can be located for consent
    B. the property is being "rehabilitated" by the occupants
    C. the state recognizes a "right to shelter"
    D. the property has really been abandoned

75. A social worker introduces herself to a family household in which an elderly man lives. The man has been reported by neighbors on several occasions for making threats of violence to a number of adolescents in the neighborhood. The worker recognizes that she is uninvited, and the BEST way for her to describe the purpose of her relationship to the family would be as

A. helping the man to modify his behavior so that no further institutional involvement will be necessary
B. helping the man to avoid the aggravating stimulus of contact with neighborhood teens
C. protecting the neighborhood from the elderly man's threats
D. arranging for the man to get counseling in order to understand and change his behavior

KEY (CORRECT ANSWERS)

1. B	16. A	31. B	46. D	61. D
2. D	17. D	32. C	47. B	62. C
3. C	18. B	33. B	48. D	63. D
4. C	19. A	34. B	49. D	64. C
5. C	20. C	35. D	50. A	65. A
6. A	21. C	36. A	51. A	66. A
7. C	22. B	37. A	52. D	67. B
8. C	23. B	38. D	53. D	68. B
9. B	24. C	39. B	54. B	69. C
10. B	25. B	40. B	55. D	70. A
11. B	26. C	41. B	56. D	71. C
12. D	27. C	42. D	57. B	72. B
13. D	28. B	43. B	58. A	73. D
14. C	29. D	44. B	59. D	74. B
15. C	30. C	45. A	60. A	75. A

TEST 2

DIRECTIONS: Each question or incomplete statement is followed by several suggested answers or completions. Select the one that BEST answers the question or completes the statement. *PRINT THE LETTER OF THE CORRECT ANSWER IN THE SPACE AT THE RIGHT.*

1. A 24-year-old mother of four, recently widowed, tells a practitioner: "I feel like my whole life has just fallen apart. I don't think I can take care of my family on my own. My husband always made all the decisions and earned the money to support us. I haven't slept well since he died and I've started drinking more often. My parents try to help me but it's not enough."
   The practitioner responds by saying: "So you're afraid about your ability to shoulder all the family responsibilities now." This response is an example of a(n)

   A. reflection
   B. clarification
   C. paraphrase
   D. summarization

   1.____

2. At the beginning of an intake interview, a social worker's tasks are to
   I. gather data and conduct an assessment
   II. establish a positive relationship with the interviewee
   III. obtain brief details that will indicate whether the situation for which the client wants help is among the problems for which the worker offers help
   IV. offer help

   A. I only
   B. I and II
   C. II and III
   D. I, II, III and IV

   2.____

3. Which of the following is NOT a basic purpose of a professional code of ethics?

   A. To provide a mechanism for professional accountability
   B. To educate professionals about sound conduct
   C. To set standards that will be understood and enforced across all cultures
   D. To serve as a tool for improving practice

   3.____

4. According to cognitive-behavioral theory, schemas represent a client's

   A. subversive attempts to persist in faulty cognitions
   B. automatic responses
   C. different response patterns
   D. core beliefs and assumptions

   4.____

5. Objective data found in a client's folder might include

   A. A neighbor's recorded statement about a previous incident
   B. Notes on an interview with his psychotherapist
   C. A work evaluation performed by a supervisor
   D. A summary of previous criminal convictions

   5.____

6. In the middle phase of a client interview, as a problem is being further explored, the practitioner should spend a considerable amount of time

   A. interpreting behavior
   B. confronting discrepancies
   C. restating or paraphrasing
   D. negotiating a service contract

7. Which of the following statements is TRUE about social work assessment?

   A. It is another term for "goal setting."
   B. It identifies a problem and its potential impact.
   C. It refers to the search for alternative solutions.
   D. It relates to the evaluation of program effectiveness.

8. An agency needs to write a proposal to a private foundation in order to request funding for renovations. It will be necessary for the agency to organize a _____ group.

   A. training
   B. task-focused
   C. recreation
   D. self-help

9. Social exchange theory is based on the idea that people

   A. often attempt to superimpose their own needs onto the desires of others
   B. aim to protect themselves from punishment in relationships
   C. aim to maximize rewards and minimize costs in relationships
   D. exchange rewards with those who are most like themselves

10. Privileged communication typically applies in cases of
    I. marital infidelity, if both spouses are participating in treatment
    II. legal proceedings in which a practitioner is asked to produce client records in court
    III. child abuse or neglect
    IV. client disclosures of personal and sensitive information

    A. I and III
    B. I, II and IV
    C. III and IV
    D. I, II, III and IV

11. During an assessment interview, a practitioner asks questions about the client's customs and traditions. The practitioner is most likely seeking information about the impact of _____ on the client's functioning.

    A. unhealthy patterns
    B. self-talk
    C. interpersonal relationships
    D. cultural diversity

12. Each of the following is true of the intervention phase of social work, EXCEPT that it

    A. is focused on problems
    B. requires interviewing, recording, letter writing, and referral skills
    C. is guided by the principles of self-determination and acceptance
    D. results naturally from a thorough assessment

13. During a client interview, a practitioner is attempting to summarize what the client has just said, but the client gives signs that he does not agree with the summary and intends to interrupt. The practitioner believes it is important for the client to hear how the summary sounds in someone else's words. In order to maintain his turn at speaking, the practitioner may want to

    A. raise an index finger
    B. raise his eyebrows
    C. speak more loudly
    D. stop all accompanying gestures and body movements

14. In Erikson's model of human development, the stage at which a child learns to meet the demands of society is

    A. identity vs. role confusion
    B. industry vs. inferiority
    C. basic trust vs. mistrust
    D. autonomy vs. shame and doubt

15. Generally, controlled experimental designs account for about _____ percent of all social work research.

    A. 5
    B. 20
    C. 35
    D. 55

16. What is the term for a social work process that brings an intervention to a close?

    A. Recognizing success
    B. Integrating gains
    C. Terminating the relationship
    D. Expanding opportunities

17. Which of the following is an example of primary prevention for mental illness?

    A. Crisis intervention
    B. Parent-child communication training
    C. Psychotherapy
    D. Teacher referrals to social workers of children targeted by bullies

18. Which of the following is an example of a closed question?

    A. How do you think you can, as you've said, 'Come more alive?'
    B. Of all the problems we've discussed, which bothers you the most?
    C. What is your relationship with your family?
    D. What kinds of things do you find yourself longing for?

19. Over time, adult personalities are likely to change in each of the following ways, EXCEPT becoming more

    A. candid
    B. dependable
    C. receptive to the company of others
    D. accepting of hardship

20. Which of the following BEST describes the mission of social work?

    A. Meeting client needs while influencing social institutions to become more responsive to people
    B. Helping clients negotiate an often complex and difficult network of services
    C. Constantly responding and adapting to social changes in micro and macro environments
    D. Identifying programs and connecting clients to needed services

21. Numerous studies have been conducted to determine which factors in a client/helping professional relationship are consistently related to positive outcomes. Which of the following is/are NOT one of these conditions?

    A. A relationship analogous to doctor/patient
    B. Empathy and positive regard
    C. A working alliance
    D. Transference and countertransference

22. A person who donates anonymously to a favorite charity is most likely driven by what Maslow called

    A. intrinsic motivation
    B. extrinsic motivation
    C. affective habituation
    D. self-actualization

23. According to the NASW code of ethics, sexual contact between practitioners and former clients is

    A. strongly discouraged under any circumstances
    B. discouraged, but considered acceptable if it occurs two years or more after the professional relationship has been terminated
    C. grounds for expulsion from the social work profession
    D. a private matter whose nature is left entirely up to the practitioner and the client

24. During an unstructured interview with a client, a practitioner generally focuses on

    A. discovering the presenting problem
    B. confronting erroneous self-talk
    C. giving reflective responses that elicit more information
    D. a prescribed list of screening questions

25. Process recording is an assessment technique that is most often used in

    A. clinical settings
    B. family sculpting

C. one-on-one interviews
D. group sessions

26. The NASW's stance on bartering with clients, rather than simply charging fees for service, includes the opinion that social workers should

   I. participate in barter in only in very limited circumstances
   II. ensure that such arrangements are an accepted practice among professionals in the local community
   III. propose bartering if it is clear the client will be unable to pay for services
   IV. never barter with clients under any circumstances

   A. I only
   B. I and II
   C. I, II and III
   D. IV only

27. Etiquette, customs, and minor regulations are examples of

   A. mores
   B. norms
   C. ethics
   D. folkways

28. A practitioner working in the Adlerian model is likely to use each of the following as an assessment instrument, EXCEPT

   A. personality inventories
   B. ecomaps
   C. lifestyle inventories
   D. early childhood recollections

29. Which of the following information would typically be solicited at the LATEST point in an intake interview?

   A. educational history
   B. family/marital/sexual history
   C. vocational history
   D. past interventions or service requests

30. According to conflict theorists, the "hidden curriculum" of schools

   A. serves to transmit different cultural values
   B. encourages social integration
   C. often results in self-fulfilling prophecy
   D. perpetuates existing social inequalities

31. The high value placed on individual freedom in American society has arguably produced each of the following, EXCEPT

   A. a cultural paradox
   B. an environmental dilemma
   C. unfair economic competition
   D. a *caveat emptor* ("let the buyer beware") approach to the market economy

32. One model of the relationship between helping professionals and clients emphasizes the social influence of professionals in counseling roles. To be effective, practitioners in the counseling role can draw on a power base that arises out of the relationship with the client. In client relationships, the power base that is typically LEAST helpful for the practitioner is known as _____ power.

    A. referent
    B. expert
    C. legitimate
    D. reward

33. In social work, experimental research designs

    A. are the most commonly conducted form of social work research
    B. obligate the researcher to offer a treatment to a control group as soon as possible after the study is terminated
    C. are usually single-system designs
    D. are generally free of ethical concerns if the research is conducted well

34. The term "social stratification" refers to social inequality that is

    A. differential
    B. structured
    C. institutionally sanctioned
    D. imperceptible

35. To a practitioner working from the behavioral perspective, the most important feature of good relationships is

    A. effective coping behaviors
    B. freedom from conflict
    C. complementary needs
    D. well-established boundaries

36. In an initial interview, it is common for clients to

    A. break down emotionally
    B. describe problems in a way that minimizes their own contributions to them
    C. disclose very personal information and emotions
    D. be someone other than the person who has arranged the interview

37. Which of the following is NOT a trend in the use of family approaches in direct social work practice?

    A. Increased attention on the family as an isolated system
    B. Increased attention to family diversity
    C. The use of a variety of social science theoretical approaches
    D. The use of multiple intervention models

38. The process whereby a client's place past feelings or attitudes toward significant people in their lives onto their social work practitioner is known as

    A. transference
    B. denial

C. countertransference
D. projection

39. Social desirability bias often causes people to

    A. make appraisals of others that are based on their social functioning rather than their effectiveness in other roles
    B. attribute their successes to skill, while blaming external factors for failures
    C. modify their responses to surveys or interviews based on what they think are desirable responses
    D. focus on the style of their interactions with others, rather than the substance

40. A social worker attends an evening anniversary party at which she has consumed some alcohol, which she rarely drinks. She doesn't think she is literally drunk, but would acknowledge feeling slightly tipsy and perhaps not in full command of herself. When she arrives at home later, she listens to a message from a client that was left on her answering machine while she was out. The client, with whom she has met several times, is feeling lonely and desperate because of the recent loss of his wife to cancer. The social worker wants to help. She should

    A. return the call immediately and try to counsel the client
    B. return the call immediately and explain that she is unable to help right now, but will call first thing tomorrow
    C. avoid contacting the client until she has recovered her ability to perform up to her usual professional standards and judgement
    D. contact a trusted colleague, give him or her the relevant information, and ask that he or she try to counsel the client over the phone

41. During an assessment interview, a practitioner asks a client: "What kinds of feelings do you have when this happens to you?" The practitioner is trying to identify the _____ associated with the problem.

    A. affect and mood states
    B. secondary gains
    C. overt behaviors or motoric responses
    D. internal dialogue

42. Hospital social workers typically engage in each of the following types of interventions or practice, EXCEPT

    A. crisis intervention
    B. discharge planning
    C. long-term counseling
    D. group work

43. For social work practitioners, symptoms of "burnout" on the job typically include each of the following, EXCEPT

    A. feeling unable to accomplish goals
    B. emotional exhaustion
    C. chronic worry
    D. a feeling of detachment from clients and work

44. When a case manager reaches the point in service coordination during which he makes a referral, he has assumed the role of

   A. evaluator
   B. broker
   C. advocate
   D. planner

45. A practitioner encounters a situation in which his own personal values conflict with a client's. In this instance, the practitioner is expected to engage in

   A. peer review
   B. value suspension
   C. legal consultation
   D. value clarification

46. Among the following American groups, the women who have the greatest risk of HIV infection are

   A. white
   B. African American
   C. Native American
   D. Hispanic

47. The trend in school social work has been a gradual shift toward an emphasis on the _____ perspective.

   A. behavioral
   B. input-based
   C. ecological
   D. psychiatric

48. The success of client-written logs as an assessment tool may depend on the client's motivation to keep a log. Which of the following is LEAST likely to help motivate a client to keep a log?

   A. Establishing a clear rationale or purpose for keeping the log
   B. Establishing negative consequences if the client fails to make log entries
   C. Adapting the log type to the client's abilities to self-monitor
   D. Involving the client in discussing and analyzing the log

49. The social work value of *empathy* is defined as a practitioner's capacity to

   A. imagine oneself in another's situation
   B. feel compassion for a person who is in distress
   C. convince a person that things will get better
   D. make a person recognize his/her own inner strength

50. Focusing on a client's positive assets and strengths during an assessment interview
    I. emphasizes the wholeness of the client system, rather than simply the problematic aspects
    II. gives a practitioner information about potential problems that might arise during an intervention
    III. helps convey to the client that they have internal resources that may prove useful
    IV. risks skewing the effectiveness of an intervention by taking the focus off the presenting problem

    A. I and III
    B. I, II and III
    C. III only
    D. I, II, III and IV

51. A hospital social worker is meeting with an 86-year-old man who suffers from Alzheimer's disease. His symptoms thus far have consisted largely of incidents of forgetfulness, and he has shown no signs of dementia or violence. The client's daughter, who has recently succeeded in having her father grant her a power of attorney over his affairs. When the social worker asks questions of the client, the daughter repeated breaks in and attempts to answer for him, though he appears to be lucid. When the social worker asks to speak to the client alone, the daughter refuses. The social worker should

    A. suspect a case of elder abuse and contact the adult protective services agency to look into it
    B. pretend to leave, and then attempt to interview the man when the daughter leaves the room
    C. suspect that the daughter may have suffered abuse at the hands of her father and adult protective services to look into it
    D. suspect a case of elder abuse and contact local law enforcement authorities

52. Which of the following is a key element of the case management paradigm?

    A. A focus on improving the quality and accessibility of resources
    B. A focus on developing vocational adjustment
    C. The selection of interventions based on empirical research
    D. Rational-emotive therapy

53. Of the following health problems, each affects the elderly to a greater extent than other age groups. The one that leads by the greatest percentage is

    A. cancer
    B. stroke
    C. heart disease
    D. Alzheimer's disease

54. Approximately _____ of all direct practice interventions are terminated because of unanticipated situational factors.

    A. an eighth
    B. a quarter
    C. half
    D. three-quarters

55. Social factors that increase the risk for suicide include each of the following, EXCEPT that the person

    A. lives alone
    B. has repeatedly rejected support
    C. has no ongoing therapeutic relationship
    D. is married

56. Practitioners are generally considered to have an ethical obligation to do each of the following, EXCEPT

    A. remain aware of their own values
    B. seek to learn about the diverse cultural backgrounds of their clients
    C. avoid imposing their values on clients
    D. refer clients whose values strongly differ from their own

57. Studies of young people who join urban gangs suggests that most often, people join gangs because of a need for a(n)

    A. peer group
    B. outlet for pent-up aggression and frustration
    C. surrogate family
    D. vehicle for criminal activity

58. After terminating a working relationship with a social worker, a client joins the local chapter of Alcoholics Anonymous. In doing so, she is attempting to

    A. form new therapeutic relationships
    B. prolong treatment
    C. maintain gains
    D. generalize gains

59. A key concept of narrative therapy is the idea tha

    A. clients often construct one-dimensional stories that don't tell the whole truth
    B. clearly naming a problem or disorder is the first step in solving it
    C. problems are inseparable from the person
    D. interventions are narrowly targeted to "revisions" of specific passages within the story

60. The creation of social service programs typically accomplishes each of the following, EXCEPT

    A. prevention
    B. enhancement
    C. retrenchment
    D. remediation

61. The most significant health problem facing Native Americans today is

    A. tuberculosis
    B. alcoholism
    C. heart disease
    D. diabetes

11 (#2)

62. Which of the following is NOT one of the six "core values" that is cited in the preamble to the NASW's code of ethics?

    A. Service
    B. Confidentiality
    C. Integrity
    D. Importance of human relationships

63. Each of the following is a guideline for a practitioner's participation in crisis intervention procedures, EXCEPT

    A. expressing empathy by saying things such as "I understand"
    B. asking the client to describe the event
    C. letting the client talk for as long as he or she likes without interruption
    D. asking the client to describe his or her reactions and responses

64. A practitioner has begun to work with clients in one-on-one settings. He thinks perhaps self-disclosure would be a good way to establish a solid, caring relationship with his clients. He should remember that in working with clients professionally, there will always be a tension between the competing forces of self-disclosure and

    A. candor
    B. liability
    C. reciprocity
    D. privacy

65. From an ethical standpoint, practitioners may
    I. accept a referral fee
    II. refer a client to a single referral source
    III. use a place of employment, such as a social services agency, to recruit clients for their own private practice
    IV. refer clients only if their problems fall outside the practitioner's area of competence

    A. I and II
    B. II only
    C. II, III and IV
    D. I, II, III and IV

66. According to Carol H. Meyer's widely used model of social work assessment, the first step in the assessment process is

    A. evaluation
    B. inferential thinking
    C. problem definition
    D. exploration

67. What is the term for the theory that explains how people generate explanations for the behaviors of others?

    A. Attribution theory
    B. Stereotyping

C. Thematic apperception
D. Implicit personality theory

68. The most important professional risk associated with amalgamating groups under very broad headings or labels, such as "Asian American," is that

   A. these terms are considered derogatory by many people
   B. most immigrants to this country proudly insist on being referred to as simply "American"
   C. many people resent being folded in to a larger group for the purpose of classification
   D. the label may obscure significant differences in the culture and experiences of individuals or subgroups within the larger category

68.____

69. Before entering a social work field placement program, prospective students are ethically entitled to know
   I. dismissal policies and procedures
   II. employment prospects for graduates
   III. the basis for performance evaluation
   IV. names and theoretical perspectives of prospective supervisors

   A. I only
   B. I, II, and III
   C. III only
   D. I, II, III and IV

69.____

70. Of the steps involved in recruitment and training at human services organizations, the FIRST typically involves

   A. reference and background checks
   B. posting position announcements
   C. screening interviews
   D. developing a job description

70.____

71. During an intake interview, a client generally avoids making eye contact with the practitioner. Averting the eyes in this way is an example of the _____ function of eye contact.

   A. monitoring
   B. expressive
   C. regulatory
   D. cognitive

71.____

72. The educational success of American children and youth is highly correlated to

   A. home schooling
   B. regional employment patterns
   C. family values
   D. race and ethnicity

72.____

73. Which of the following techniques is a client-centered practitioner MOST likely to use?

   A. Response shaping
   B. Reflection

73.____

C. Giving advice
D. Analysis

74. During a meeting with a client who has just ended his marriage after twelve years, the client insists repeatedly that everything is fine. No matter what the practitioner asks or tries to suggest, the response is the same. The client is engaging in the facial management technique known as

A. neutralizing
B. masking
C. intensifying
D. deintensifying

75. A practitioner is considering a dual relationship with a client. Before forming such a relationship, the practitioner should consider
    I. divergent responsibilities
    II. incompatible expectations
    III. the power differential
    IV. referring the client to another practitioner

A. I and II
B. I, II and III
C. II, III and IV
D. I, II, III and IV

KEY (CORRECT ANSWERS)

1. A	16. B	31. A	46. B	61. B
2. C	17. B	32. D	47. C	62. B
3. C	18. B	33. B	48. B	63. A
4. D	19. C	34. B	49. A	64. D
5. D	20. A	35. A	50. B	65. B
6. C	21. A	36. B	51. A	66. D
7. B	22. A	37. A	52. A	67. A
8. B	23. A	38. A	53. C	68. D
9. C	24. C	39. C	54. C	69. B
10. B	25. C	40. C	55. D	70. D
11. D	26. B	41. A	56. D	71. C
12. A	27. D	42. C	57. C	72. D
13. C	28. A	43. C	58. C	73. B
14. B	29. B	44. B	59. A	74. A
15. A	30. D	45. B	60. C	75. B

EXAMINATION SECTION
TEST 1

DIRECTIONS: Each question or incomplete statement is followed by several suggested answers or completions. Select the one the BEST answers the question or completes the statement. *PRINT THE LETTER OF THE CORRECT ANSWER IN THE SPACE AT THE RIGHT.*

1. At the outset of treatment, a client tells the social worker that she must promise never to involuntarily hospitalize her, no matter how depressed or suicidal she may seem. In formulating a response to this request, the social worker should use the underlying ethical principle of

    A. the need to do whatever is necessary to maintain a therapeutic relationship with a client
    B. never making a promise that is in conflict with legal and ethical requirements
    C. the client"s right to self-determination
    D. the understanding that the client has legitimate, defensible reasons for making this request

1.____

2. For a Gestalt therapist, a primary goal of treatment is to help the client

    A. integrate the present with his/her past and future
    B. develop a "success identity"
    C. integrate the functioning of his/her mind and body
    D. incorporate the external into the internal

2.____

3. What is the term for a social system that is part of a larger system and made up of several smaller systems?

    A. Focal system
    B. Schema
    C. Holon
    D. Gemeinschaft

3.____

4. The most commonly occurring psychological disorders are _____ disorders.

    A. Dissociative
    B. Psychosexual
    C. Mood
    D. Somatoform

4.____

5. In the early stages of problem-solving communication training with a family, the practitioner should FIRST assess

    A. family cognitions about communication/arguments
    B. the history of the problem
    C. family assets
    D. specific skill deficits

5.____

6. An intern at an agency for the chronically mentally ill meets with a 24-year-old client who has been referred by his family doctor. The primary basis for this referral is the client's isolation from peers and general lack of social skills. In many ways, the client reminds the intern of the quiet, studious friends she made in graduate school, who had very little time to socialize because of studies and part-time jobs. The client tells the intern he doesn't think he belongs in this place, and she silently agrees, though her supervisor and more experienced workers seem to believe that this is the right place for him. In her assessment of this client's situation, the intern has relied on the _____ heuristic.

   A. theoretical
   B. schematic
   C. availability
   D. representativeness

7. Which of the following types of feminism proposes that men and women have different values due to the structure of sex and gender roles in society?

   A. socialist
   B. reactionary
   C. radical
   D. liberal

8. The most significant problem with establishing "comparable worth" at an agency is that

   A. males and females may use different strategies to reach the same decision or solution
   B. the job evaluation techniques themselves may be gender-biased
   C. job evaluation techniques are not as useful for very complex jobs
   D. it is difficult to compare achievement across different domains

9. A social worker decides that solution-focused therapy is the most appropriate approach for a family that has come to see her about financial problems. The social worker's FIRST intervention would be to

   A. discuss time constraints and make sure the family knows the intervention will be brief
   B. get a clear picture of how the system functions
   C. get a history of the origins of the symptoms
   D. discuss how things would be for the family if the problem was already solved

10. Social service agencies, in attempting to make a certain program more efficient and useful, may sometimes get lost in pursuing a prescribed means of service delivery at the expense of accomplishing program goals. This is known as

    A. output loss
    B. goal displacement
    C. bounded rationality
    D. organizational shaping

11. According to Elkind, the most significant descriptor of adolescent thought is

    A. concrete
    B. irrational

C. egocentric
D. moralistic

12. In a program evaluation, which type of data is concerned primarily with whether or not the program goals are being met?

    A. throughput
    B. process
    C. product
    D. input

13. Which of the following problems or disorders is LEAST likely to be changed through psychotherapy?

    A. Anorexia nervosa
    B. Conduct disorder
    C. Antisocial personality disorder
    D. Compulsive behavior

14. The record-keeping requirements at a typical social services agency require the completion of a review treatment plan at an interval no longer than

    A. after every client contact
    B. weekly
    C. every 30 days
    D. every 90 days

15. For social workers, it is usually most appropriate to view a woman's separation from an abusive husband as

    A. a series of losses which initiates a mourning process
    B. a solution that must be accomplished as quickly as possible
    C. a partial process at best if children are involved
    D. the best of all possible solutions to the problem of domestic abuse

16. Formative policy research at social services agencies

    A. is usually conducted in response to legislative mandates
    B. focuses on policy development rather than on its impact on clients and agencies
    C. identifies social policy as the independent variable
    D. is based entirely on output goals

17. Abusive families are most often characterized by

    A. openness and affection
    B. rigid boundaries and clear roles
    C. a strong parental subsystem
    D. denial and enmeshed boundaries

18. The principal assessment tool for clinicians working from the intergenerational perspective on the family is the

    A. life cycle matrix
    B. social history

C. genogram
D. ecomap

19. The "output goals" of a social service program are MOST likely to include

    A. specified ratings of services by clients on a standardized scale
    B. observable effects on a given community or clientele
    C. the number of units of service provided
    D. the number of clients served

20. A 35-year-old client, a high school teacher, reports to a practitioner at an outpatient clinic and reports the following incident: he, a high school teacher, was in the middle of a lesson during a class period that had been particularly difficult for him over the past several months, because the class was large and often noisy. During the middle of today's lesson, the client suddenly began to sweat profusely and his heart started to race. He continued with the lesson but soon felt dizzy and fearful that he was about to die. The feeling was so overwhelming that he had to leave the class unattended and retreat to the teacher's lounge, where he was found sitting alone and trembling. The client's physician has found no evidence of medical problems. The most likely DSM-IV diagnosis for this client would be

    A. panic disorder
    B. posttraumatic stress disorder
    C. dissociative disorder
    D. social phobia

21. Which of the following statements reveals a client with a formal-operational emotional orientation?

    A. I'm so sad right now that my stomach hurts. I haven't eaten all day.
    B. I suppose there are two different ways of looking at this. On one hand, these arguments are really painful, but I know I have to set limits for my son and it's part of my role as a parent. I know he needs to find his own space, but his decisions are sometimes questionable.
    C. I feel great about the new relationship I'm in. I think I've met the perfect man.
    D. As I think about it, I feel bad because it seems as if we've been arguing a lot lately. It's almost a ritual--every time I get ready to leave the house, an argument starts.

22. The purpose of the mental status examination in psychotherapy is

    A. personality testing
    B. to make a diagnosis
    C. reality testing
    D. to determine the severity of psychotic symptoms

23. Which of the following interviewing skills is most useful for discovering the deeply held thoughts and feelings underlying the client's experience?

    A. Confrontation
    B. Open-ended questioning
    C. Focusing
    D. Reflection of meaning

24. A client who has a history of hypomanic and major depressive episodes would have a diagnosis of

    A. Hypomanic disorder
    B. Cyclothymic disorder
    C. Bipolar I disorder
    D. Bipolar II disorder

25. Which of the following theoretical frameworks establishes equity and distributive justice as its ideal ends of development

    A. Behavioral/social exchange
    B. Ego psychology
    C. Symbolic interactionism
    D. Structural functionalism

26. A "Theory X" manager in an organization is likely to

    A. adopt a team approach to problem-solving
    B. use tangible rewards and sanctions to shape employee behavior
    C. work to set up and maintain a work environment that promotes growth and creativity
    D. assume that subordinates want to work toward organization goal attainment

27. Which of the following is generally NOT recommended as part of an intervention with a Native American client who follows older traditions?

    A. Serving food
    B. Emphasizing the past
    C. Giving gifts
    D. Including friends and family

28. The process of transforming a piece of legislation into a specific program or policy, by means of identifying specific guidelines and operating procedures to be used in administering the program, is known as

    A. rationalization
    B. promulgation
    C. consignment
    D. confederation

29. Which of the following is NOT an ego-defense mechanism?

    A. Regression
    B. Reality testing
    C. Displacement
    D. Sublimation

30. Which of the following is probably the MOST appropriate candidate for an intensive, heterogeneous outpatient therapy group?

    A. A paranoid person
    B. A person with bipolar II disorder

C. An alcoholic or drug addict
D. A person with brain damage

31. In removing intracultural barriers to achievement for clients of color, interventions should be aimed at

    A. active encouragement of family involvement
    B. recognition and affirmation of client system strengths
    C. changes in institutional policies, practices, and administration
    D. improved educational/vocational opportunities through greater teacher/employer awareness of diversity, history and customs

32. Which of the following is a means-tested program?

    A. Medicare
    B. Social Security
    C. Public education
    D. Police protection

33. One of the greatest risks associated with too little self-disclosure in the group therapy process is

    A. severely limited reality testing
    B. low group cohesiveness
    C. yielding an inappropriate amount of member control
    D. severe dependence

34. In behavioral therapy, the systematic desensitization process, usually performed by disassociating a neutral stimulus from a situation that has created fear or anxiety, is also known as

    A. extinction
    B. aversion therapy
    C. overcorrection
    D. counterconditioning

35. The primary function of reflecting feelings during a client interview is to

    A. help the client sort out mixed or ambivalent feelings
    B. grounding the worker and client in concrete experience
    C. bring out additional details of the client's emotional world
    D. make implicit, sometimes hidden emotions clear to the client

36. Which of the following is NOT a privileged relationship during the prosecution of child abuse?

    A. Priest-confessor
    B. Lawyer-client
    C. Psychotherapist-patient
    D. Physician-patient

37. According to ego psychology, the ego

A. mediates between erotic energies and superego constraints
B. is a drive for pleasure
C. imposes a set of rules to control unbridled pleasure-seeking
D. offers ideals for the individual to strive for

38. Which of the following statements reveals a discrepancy that is external to the speaker?

    A. I don't mind talking about that at all.
    B. I wanted to go to business school, but my grades weren't good enough.
    C. My mother is a saint, but she doesn't respect me.
    D. This is a nice office. It's too bad it's in this neighborhood.

39. During an intake interview for a woman who has committed a violent crime, the clinician notes that whenever the woman talks of the act she does so without any emotion—anger, shame, guilt, or sadness—whatsoever. From the psychoanalytic perspective, the woman is using the defense mechanism of

    A. isolation
    B. fantasy formation
    C. repression
    D. rationalization

40. A humanist, looking at an individual's misbehavior, would conclude that a person who acts badly is

    A. suffering from a kind of illness
    B. experiencing a detachment from her moral compass
    C. willfully disregarding the norms which characterize her community
    D. reacting to the deprivation of her basic needs

41. Clinicians in private practice are generally paid for
    I. direct services to clients
    II. number of hours on the job
    III. indirect services

    A. I only
    B. I and II
    C. II only
    D. I, II and III

42. A clinician is meeting with a transactional group for the first time and works intensely at studying the members and their transactions. In the early stages of work with this group, the clinician's greatest challenge is likely to be

    A. defusing conflict between members
    B. identifying the self-talk or cognitions that lie behind a transaction
    C. heading off the tendency toward subgroupings
    D. determining which ego state a transaction comes from

43. A social worker has been seeing a client for several months and has developed a good working relationship. The client loses her job and cannot afford to pay for therapy. Under the social worker's professional code and value system, the BEST option in this case would be to

A. refer the client to low-cost therapy from another provider
B. allow the client to divert payments until she gets another job
C. provide the therapy free of charge until the client can find employment
D. reduce the fee for this client and/or offer her shorter sessions

44. "Acceptance" in the therapeutic relationship mean that the practitioner

    I. separates the client from her behavior
    II. indicates approval of the client's behavior
    III. expresses sympathy for the client
    IV. demonstrates tolerance for client's behavior

    A. I only
    B. I and II
    C. II, III and IV
    D. I, II, III and IV

45. According to Papernow, most people first enter a stepfamily with

    A. a clear awareness of the reality of their situation
    B. a growing sense of realistic intimacy with new family members
    C. the fantasy that they will rescue the new partner and any children from the deficiencies of a previous marriage
    D. a feeling of resentment toward new family members who place new demands on their time, money, and other resources

46. An ideal therapeutic relationship in social work is one that

    A. connects the client with the proper support services
    B. allows and helps the client's capacity to work out his own issues
    C. is an ongoing source of support
    D. the client can rely upon as a problem-solving tool

47. Which of the following is NOT characteristic of a clinician who is conducting reality therapy with a client?

    A. Viewing mental illness labels as destructive
    B. Focusing on behavior rather than feelings
    C. Discouraging value judgements
    D. Not offering sympathy

48. In general, a DSM-IV diagnosis of a specific disorder includes a criterion of

    A. no medical involvement
    B. a clinically significant impairment or distress in a social or occupational area
    C. an identifiable etiology
    D. distress that has exceeded a period of 8 weeks

49. A client interview is interrupted by a long silence that makes the social worker uncomfortable. The FIRST thing the social worker should do is

    A. inform the client that of his/her (the worker's) discomfort and observe the client's reaction
    B. restate the last words spoken by the client

C. say, "I wonder why you're so quiet"
D. study the client to see if he/she appears comfortable with the silence

50. A social worker is seeing a Latino family that immigrated to the United States several years ago. The social worker is not Latino. The family often arrive late for their sessions, causing some scheduling problems—and mild annoyance—for the social worker. The best way for the social worker to handle this would be to

    A. be aware that time may be perceived differently in their culture and invite them to discuss what being late means to them
    B. understand that being late is probably an expression of cultural resistance to disclosing family issues
    C. be aware that time may be perceived differently in their culture, and take a more flexible approach to beginning scheduled sessions
    D. consider referring the family to a Hispanic therapist

51. The foundation of clinical supervisory techniques—and the focus of supervision—is/are typically

    A. case material
    B. educational assessment
    C. long-term practitioner development goals
    D. practitioner attitudes and values

52. A practitioner grew up as the oldest child of alcoholic parents, and was often placed in the role of parent to his three younger siblings. In order to establish solid therapeutic relationships with his clients, the most important challenge this practitioner will probably face is

    A. being able to trust that clients have the capacity to work through their problems
    B. being able to see clearly the problems faced by alcoholic clients
    C. the risk that he will impose an undue level of responsibility on clients early in the intervention process
    D. a lack of faith in his ability to help clients change

53. A married couple and their two teenage sons see a clinician for the first time for help with what they view as an unhealthy spirit of competition between the two boys. The clinician observes the family's interactions and characterizes them as high-functioning and relatively flexible. Which of the following models of intervention is probably MOST appropriate for this family?

    A. Structural-functional
    B. Strategic
    C. Experiential
    D. Solution-focused

54. According to the lifespan perspective of human development and behavior, development is NOT

    A. contextual
    B. historically embedded
    C. unidirectional
    D. lifelong

55. The sole motivation for a client's feigning illness in factitious disorder is to

   A. obtain prescription drugs
   B. draw attention away from his/her psychological problems
   C. assume a sick role.
   D. escape material and everyday responsibilities

56. In school, an 8-year-old boy has considerably impaired social interactions with other children, along with severely impaired language skills. The boy also pulls at his hair constantly, sometimes leaving ragged bald patches, and often bites himself, leaving wounds and scars that his parents have made the primary concern for treatment. Appropriate diagnoses for this boy include
   I. Asperger's disorder
   II. Stereotypic movement disorder
   III. Autism
   IV. Mental retardation

   A. I and II
   B. II and III
   C. III only
   D. IV only

57. In order to ensure a margin of error no greater than 5%, what is the size of the sample required to represent a population of 10,000?

   A. 108
   B. 370
   C. 1235
   D. 9,500

58. Social learning theory recognizes each of the following as a key factor in human development, EXCEPT

   A. cognition
   B. heredity
   C. behavior
   D. environment

59. According to Annon, clients in sex therapy need interventions at very specific levels. The first of these levels is

   A. specific suggestions
   B. intensive therapy
   C. limited information
   D. permission

60. Which of the following is named as the etiological agent for adjustment disorder?

   A. Depressed mood
   B. Stress
   C. Sudden trauma
   D. Organic chemistry imbalance

61. Social workers generally observe several distinct characteristics in the life cycle of poor African-American families. Which of the following is NOT one of these?

    A. Households that are frequently female-headed and isolated from the community
    B. A scarceness of resources that compels a reliance on government institutions
    C. A truncated life cycle with less time to resolve developmental tasks
    D. A life cycle punctuated by numerous unpredictable life events

62. A 50-year-old client has been significantly depressed for more than a year. For the past two months, the client has been convinced that he has developed lung cancer. The most appropriate DSM-IV diagnosis for the client would be

    A. conversion disorder
    B. major depressive episode
    C. somatoform disorder, not otherwise specified
    D. hypochondriasis

63. Persuasive arguments for flexible-rate fee schedules include
    I. Services more accessible to disadvantaged clients
    II. Endorsements of insurers and other third-party organizations
    III. No means testing
    IV. Consistency with consumer protection laws

    A. I only
    B. I and III
    C. I, II and IV
    D. I, II, III and IV

64. The psychoanalytical perspective views _____ as the most powerful and pervasive defense mechanism.

    A. projection
    B. rationalization
    C. repression
    D. denial

65. Which of the following approaches to client interviewing is MOST likely to make use of interpretation or refraining?

    A. Psychodynamic
    B. Solution-focused
    C. Client-centered
    D. Behavioral

66. When a clinician is on a provider panel for a managed health care company, he or she:

    A. is guaranteed a certain number of referrals from this company per year.
    B. has met the qualifications for company, and has no guarantee of referrals.
    C. agree to see any referral within your specialty.
    D. will receive a full fee from the company when he/she sees a client

67. When a therapeutic relationship is functioning on the cognitive level, the therapist will probably engage in each of the following processes, EXCEPT

A. highlighting inconsistencies
B. reassuring
C. refraining
D. asking key questions

68. Several days after losing her job, a woman becomes so depressed that she is unable to get out of bed until well into the afternoon, and rarely leaves her home. By the time she reports to a practitioner for treatment, she has been depressed and had trouble sleeping for about 4 months. The most appropriate DSM-IV diagnosis for this client is

    A. major depressive episode
    B. dysthmic disorder
    C. adjustment disorder with depressed mood
    D. depressive disorder, not otherwise specified

69. The NASW code's prohibition of dual relationships is most likely to be challenged by social workers who

    A. are part of an interdisciplinary team
    B. live and work in rural areas
    C. are involved in direct practice
    D. perform supervisory functions

70. Many practitioners make use of informal assessment instruments such as self-reporting questionnaires, indexes, and profiles. The main risk associated with these instruments as assessment tools is that they

    A. often put the client on the defensive
    B. may place too much emphasis on relatively unimportant details
    C. suggest that the practitioner may be lazy or incompetent
    D. often provoke client dissembling

71. The term "active listening" mostly refers to a person's ability to

    A. indicate with numerous physical cues that he/she is listening
    B. take an active role in determining which information is provided by the client
    C. concentrate on what is being said
    D. both listen to the client and accomplish other meaningful tasks at the same time

72. Which of the following is a latent function of the family unit?

    A. Economic production
    B. Socialization of children
    C. Provision of emotional support to members
    D. Contribution to institutional arrangements

73. Current knowledge of post-traumatic stress disorder (PTSD) indicates that if the initial stage of anxiety and obsession with the trauma persist for longer than _____, the patient then enters stage 2, or acute PTSD.

    A. 5-10 days
    B. 4-6 weeks
    C. 8-12 weeks
    D. 3-6 months

74. After making contact with a person in crisis and establishing a relationship, a clinician faces the task of examining the dimensions of the problem, in order to define it. Which of the following is NOT typically a task of this phase of crisis intervention?

    A. Exploring alternatives
    B. Assessing the dangerousness or lethality of the situation
    C. Identifying the precipitating event that led to the crisis
    D. Detailing a client's previous coping methods

75. In general, administrative evaluation at a social services agency differs from practice evaluation in that administrative evaluation is

    A. external to the supervisory relationship
    B. continuous
    C. basically self-contained
    D. specific

KEY (CORRECT ANSWERS)

1. B	16. B	31. A	46. B	61. A
2. C	17. D	32. A	47. C	62. B
3. C	18. C	33. A	48. B	63. A
4. C	19. C	34. D	49. D	64. C
5. D	20. A	35. D	50. A	65. A
6. D	21. D	36. D	51. A	66. B
7. A	22. C	37. A	52. A	67. B
8. B	23. D	38. B	53. D	68. C
9. D	24. D	39. A	54. C	69. B
10. B	25. A	40. D	55. C	70. B
11. C	26. B	41. A	56. B	71. C
12. C	27. B	42. D	57. B	72. D
13. C	28. B	43. D	58. B	73. B
14. D	29. B	44. A	59. D	74. A
15. A	30. B	45. C	60. B	75. A

TEST 2

DIRECTIONS: Each question or incomplete statement is followed by several suggested answers or completions. Select the one the BEST answers the question or completes the statement. *PRINT THE LETTER OF THE CORRECT ANSWER IN THE SPACE AT THE RIGHT.*

1. An 18-year-old girl is brought into a hospital emergency room by her family, who reported that she experienced sudden blindness. She had been arguing with her mother about why her mother was so much stricter with her than her father, when her mother suddenly blurted out that she and the father were seeking a divorce. The girl continued to argue for several minutes but then suddenly stopped and announced that she couldn't see anything. An examination reveals no neurological deficits. The client should most likely receive a diagnosis of   1.____

   A. conversion disorder
   B. somatoform disorder, not otherwise specified
   C. dissociative disorder
   D. hypochondriasis

2. An important difference between brief psychotherapy and crisis intervention is that   2.____

   A. brief therapy focuses on pathology
   B. crisis intervention focuses on specific issues
   C. brief therapy focuses on specific issues
   D. crisis intervention focuses on pathology

3. During an evaluation session in which the supervisor and practitioner are discussing the progress of the practitioner's current caseload, the practitioner admits to being unhappy with the overall progress of his clients, but attributes it to problems he has been experiencing because of excessive pressure placed on him by the supervisor. At this point in the evaluation, the supervisor should   3.____

   A. reassure the practitioner that whatever pressures have been placed on him have been for the benefit of his professional development
   B. apologize and suggest that the practitioner think of ways in which the supervisory relationship can be made more comfortable
   C. try to steer the focus of the discussion toward client progress
   D. remind the practitioner that he is the one ultimately responsible for handling the pressures that come with social work practice

4. In the time series design of program evaluation, the primary threat to internal validity is   4.____

   A. history
   B. selection
   C. testing
   D. regression to the mean

5. A client tells her clinician that members of an international espionage ring are after her to torture her and find out what she knows. She suspects that there are higher forces at work behind her persecution, but she can't tell the clinician what these forces are. Her beliefs have interfered with her work and social life for more than a year. The most appropriate diagnosis for this client is   5.____

A. psychotic disorder, not otherwise specified
B. schizophrenia, paranoid type
C. delusional disorder
D. schizoaffective disorder

6. Which of the following factors is NOT typically associated with ethnicity?

   A. Language
   B. Physical type
   C. Economic status
   D. Culture

7. A 19-year-old male client's father calls the social worker and requests information about his son's treatment. In this situation, the social worker should

   A. confirm that the son is in treatment but give no other information
   B. tell the father about his son's progress but not reveal any specifics
   C. set up a conjoint therapy session
   D. refuse to reveal any information

8. In an approach-avoidance conflict, as the person nears the goal,

   A. attraction and aversion both increase
   B. attraction and aversion both decrease
   C. attraction increases and aversion decreases
   D. atraction decreases and aversion increases

9. According the Herzberg's model of employee motivation, which of the following is a "hygiene" factor?

   A. Potential for growth
   B. Interesting, challenging work
   C. Freedom
   D. Salary

10. A disturbance of consciousness accompanied by some changes in cognition is the distinguishing feature of

    A. schizophrenia
    B. dementia
    C. delusion
    D. delirium

11. Public and private social service agencies generally differ in each of the following ways, EXCEPT

    A. practitioner certification requirements
    B. philosophy of service
    C. service eligibility requirements
    D. scope of services

12. Consistently, an employee is observed to be extremely friendly toward his boss, whom he really despises. From a Freudian perspective, the employee is exhibiting

A. reaction formation
B. isolation of affect
C. projection
D. sublimation

13. The purpose of an explanatory design for practice evaluation is to

    A. determine the causes of specific client behaviors
    B. examine and reflect on the intervention being used
    C. examine the impact of the intervention on the target behavior
    D. monitor client progress

14. Which of the following neurotransmitters or neuropeptides is generally deficient in clients with anorexia nervosa?

    A. Serotonin
    B. Cholecystokinin
    C. Dopamine
    D. Neuropeptide Y

15. Services that are provided to clients without a means test are described as

    A. pro-rated
    B. contributory
    C. eclectic
    D. universal

16. In a family intervention formed in the strategic model, a clinician who uses a "restraining strategy" will begin the intervention by

    A. warning the family of the danger of continuing its symptomatic behavior
    B. directing the family to stop its symptomatic behavior
    C. warning the family of the negative consequences of behavioral change
    D. instructing the family to engage in only nonsymptomatic behavior

17. The primary disadvantage associated with purchase-of-service agreements in social services is

    A. higher agency costs
    B. further fragmentation of the social service system
    C. decreased innovation in problem-solving
    D. diminished scope of services

18. Roles in the alcoholic family system have been labeled by Wegscheider and others. Typically, the youngest child in an alcoholic family occupies the role of

    A. mascot
    B. lost child
    C. hero
    D. scapegoat

19. The primary purpose for using confrontation in a client interview is to

A. teach mediation and conflict resolution skills
B. activate the client's potential for change
C. identify mixed messages in behaviors and thoughts or feelings
D. identify the processes the client uses to make changes

20. A clinician at a mental health clinic decides to work from the perspective of Rogers client-centered therapy. If the counselor goes against the policy of the clinic and decides to reject the use of diagnosis, it will be because from the person-centered perspective,

    A. the validity of diagnostic labels has not been empirically demonstrated
    B. diagnosis forces the therapist, rather than the client, to assume the expert role
    C. labeling results in an incongruence between self and experience
    D. labeling discourages the process of in-depth interpretation of the client's behavior

21. Which of the following interventions is one of the most frequently used therapies in the treatment of phobias?

    A. Exposure therapy
    B. Object relations
    C. Extinction
    D. Social skills training

22. Which of the following statements about therapeutic group composition is generally FALSE?

    A. Task groups that are homogeneous are less productive and cohesive than heterogeneous groups.
    B. Homogeneous groups of task-oriented, high-structure, impersonal people function as effective, change-producing human relations groups.
    C. Heterogeneous encounter groups are more effective in producing greater self-actualization of members.
    D. Homogeneous groups of person-oriented, low-structure people do not generally function as effective human relations groups.

23. When behaviors are known and categorized prior to an observation, and the intention is to collect quantitative data, the method of choice is

    A. structured observation
    B. the Likert scale
    C. participant observation
    D. structured interview

24. A client who was abused as a child, whenever speaking of her parents, tends to cast the father in the most negative light possible, describing his as evil and every encounter with him as a disaster. Of her mother, however, she has only the most glowing praise, often referring to her as a saint. From a psychodynamic perspective, the client is using the defense mechanism known as

    A. reaction formation
    B. primitive idealization
    C. projection
    D. splitting

25. In the transactional analysis model of social intercourse, the safest type of interaction is

    A. a game
    B. intimate
    C. ritualistic
    D. a pastime

26. Dissociative amnesia is usually
    I.   related to the inability to recall important personal information
    II. retrograde
    III. selective
    IV. accompanied by apraxia

    A. I and II
    B. II and III
    C. I, II and III
    D. II, III and IV

27. People often have difficulty receiving information because of an impairment or other barrier. Which of these will probably NOT help such a person to better understand a message?

    A. Repeating the message
    B. Changing the sequence of the message
    C. Changing the form in which the message is transmitted
    D. Using an interpreter

28. A social worker is working with an autistic child who is mute. The major goal of intervention is the development of language. The social worker begins by rewarding the child with food whenever he vocalizes. The social worker then begins to reward the child only when his vocalizations occur within ten seconds of the social worker's vocalization, then only if the child's vocalizations resemble the social worker's, and so on, until the child's vocalizations are identical to those of the social worker. The technique is used until the child is eventually using words and sentences. This technique is known as:

    A. counterconditioning
    B. chaining
    C. shaping
    D. prompting

29. Potential limitations on confidentiality should be discussed with a client

    A. when the social worker determines it to be appropriate
    B. at the onset of the professional relationship
    C. at the onset of the professional relationship and thereafter as needed
    D. and documented in writing as soon as possible

30. Other than describing a client's problem in a way that imposes meaning on a large amount of information, the primary cognitive task of assessment is to

    A. establish client comfort with the therapeutic plan
    B. selectively focus on the information that will be most useful to the treatment planning process

C. infer whether a specific groups of facts or observations belongs to a larger known category of problems
D. identify the client's feelings of concern

31. The status of the practitioner/client therapeutic relationship is seen as an important aspect of therapy in each of the following models, EXCEPT

    A. ecosystems
    B. psychoanalysis
    C. client-centered
    D. behavioral

32. Among the skills important to effective communication with clients, the most sophisticated and complex is/are

    A. encouraging, paraphrasing, and summarization
    B. confrontation
    C. influencing skills
    D. open and closed questions

33. The _____ approach to human behavior attempts to describe behaviors in ways that allow for generalization across cultures.

    A. etic
    B. holistic
    C. emic
    D. pluralist

34. The most widely-used bivariate statistical measure in social work is

    A. regression analysis
    B. cross-tabulation
    C. slope/drift
    D. correlation

35. Which of the following statements is most abstract?

    A. Last night my mother told me I was a disappointment.
    B. I cry all day long. I can't eat.
    C. My daughter just sent me a letter.
    D. My family is very close.

36. Each of the following is viewed by clinicians as an important element of the therapeutic relationship, EXCEPT

    A. confidentiality
    B. dependability
    C. sympathy
    D. confidence

37. The _____ theory of human development holds that human behavior is strongly influenced by biology, is tied to evolution, and is characterized by critical and sensitive periods.

A. Biosocial
B. Ecological
C. Social learning
D. Ethological

38. The residual model of social welfare
    I. is developed piecemeal as a reaction to the development of social problems, rather than in anticipation of them
    II. views government as the last line of defense for people experiencing problems
    III. views family and work as the first line of defense
    IV. expects individuals to have trouble meeting the needs of modern living

    A. I only
    B. I and II
    C. I, II, and III
    D. I, II, III and IV

39. One of the helping models for multiproblem families is the Multiple-Impact Family-Therapy (MIFT) model, which includes each of the following elements, EXCEPT

    A. a long-term, client-centered approach
    B. an extended session format
    C. use of a team of professionals who work directly with the family
    D. immediate response to a request for service

40. Which of the following has NOT been a factor in the recent growth of the for-profit sector of social services in the United States?

    A. The ability of for-profit agencies to offer more stable financial sources of income than other investments
    B. The historical ability of private-sector solutions to solve problems that the government has failed to solve
    C. The growing complexity and number of problems experienced by the disadvantaged
    D. The existence of for-profit opportunities outside of public health insurance benefits

41. Which of the following is NOT typically a factor used by private clinicians to determine fees for clients?

    A. The amount charged by local psychiatrists of equal experience
    B. What the worker thinks will be the most attractive rate to the clientele she hopes to attract
    C. What third-party financing organizations identify as reasonable and customary charges
    D. How much other helping professionals charge for such services

42. Erikson's final stage of psychosocial development, experienced during late adulthood, is

    A. industry vs. inferiority
    B. generativity vs. stagnation
    C. intimacy vs. isolation
    D. integrity vs. despair

43. Which of the following approaches to social services policymaking assess the process of moving from the identification of a social problem to implementing a policy and assessing the impact the policy has on the original problem?

    A. Prescriptive
    B. Investment
    C. Cause and consequences
    D. Formative

44. Research suggests that negative emotional effects from divorce are LEAST likely to impact

    A. women who do not remarry
    B. women who remarry
    C. men who do not remarry
    D. men who remarry

45. Closed questions typically do NOT begin with the word

    A. how
    B. is
    C. do
    D. are

46. In order to receive a diagnosis of acute stress disorder that conforms to DSM-IV standards, a client's symptoms must occur within _____ of a traumatic event.

    A. 5 days
    B. 4 weeks
    C. 3 months
    D. 6 months

47. Which of the following types of programs is typically administered exclusively at the county level?

    A. Food stamps
    B. AFDC
    C. Medical assistance
    D. General assistance

48. In the clinical supervision of a social work practitioner, a good general policy is to

    A. begin with technical skill learning and then move to theoretical and perspective learning
    B. begin with perspective learning and then move to technical skill learning
    C. teach a supervisee technical skills and theory simultaneously
    D. avoid both technical skills and theory and instead focus on smaller, concrete problems faced by the practitioner

49. Approximately what percentage of child maltreatment/abuse cases involve sexual abuse?

    A. 5   B. 10   C. 30   D. 50

50. In the United States, most social policy is formulated

   A. by individual agency boards
   B. in a de facto manner by the direct practice of social workers
   C. through legislation
   D. by state boards

51. Which of the following terms is used to describe memory loss that has a purely psychological cause?

   A. Anterograde
   B. Organic
   C. Retrograde
   D. Inorganic

52. Which of the following statements reveals a client with a sensorimotor emotional orientation?

   A. A lot of us are angry. I know my boss is busy, but his forgetting to sign the payroll is going to cost some of us our weekend plans.
   B. I'm feeling lost I start to tremble when I go out in public.
   C. It seems that every time my wife is late meeting me somewhere, I get really angry with her. My time is valuable.
   D. I feel really angry because my best friend borrowed my car without asking.

53. In order to receive a diagnosis of adjustment disorder that conforms to DSM-IV standards, a client's symptoms must occur within _____ of a traumatic event

   A. 5 days
   B. 4 weeks
   C. 3 months
   D. 6 months

54. In the static-group comparison design of program evaluation, the primary threat to external validity is

   A. maturation-treatment interaction
   B. selection-treatment interaction
   C. reactive effects
   D. history-treatment interaction

55. According to Ainsworth, a "Type B" baby

   A. exhibits insecurity by avoiding the mother
   B. exhibits insecurity by resisting the mother
   C. exhibits insecurity by clinging to the mother
   D. uses the mother as a secure base from which to explore the environment

56. Which of the following is a primary social work setting?

A. Community center
B. Child protective services agency
C. Hospital
D. Nursing home

57. A client is a 40-year-old man who works as a night custodian at a local bank building. He keeps to himself and seems to have no interests outside his job, his stamp collection, and his two cats. He lives alone in a small apartment, has no close friends, and appears to have to interest in making friends. If this client is to receive a DSM-IV diagnosis, what would it be?

    A. Avoidant personality disorder
    B. Schizoid personality disorder
    C. Antisocial personality disorder
    D. No diagnosis—the man's isolation is not a disorder

58. A social or financial service that requires an applicant to prove financial need in order to receive the service is described as

    A. means-tested
    B. prescriptive
    C. residual
    D. eclectic

59. The initial aim in treating a client with conversion disorder is

    A. removal of the symptom
    B. determining predisposing factors
    C. forming a description of interpersonal relationships
    D. discovering precipitating stressors

60. Which of the following is NOT a preexperimental design for program evaluation?

    A. One-group pretest/posttest
    B. Client satisfaction surveys
    C. Static-group comparison
    D. Solomon four-group approach

61. In their definition of "family," many Asian Americans, especially Chinese Americans, are likely to include
    I.   members of the nuclear family
    II. members of the extended family
    III. the informal network of community relations
    IV. all their ancestors and descendants

    A. I and II
    B. I, II and III
    C. I, II and IV
    D. I, II, III and IV

62. Within the context of the therapeutic relationship, practitioners and clients deal either explicitly or implicitly with
    I. past experiences that have affected abilities to relate to others
    II. the present physical, emotional, and perceptual state of the transaction
    III. each person's expectations of the process

    A. I only
    B. I and II
    C. II and III
    D. I, II and II

63. Assertiveness and social skills training are interventions MOST likely to be useful to clients with

    A. panic disorder with agoraphobia
    B. avoidant personality disorder
    C. narcissistic personality disorder
    D. schizoid personality disorder

64. A client reports to a practitioner at an outpatient care clinic in clear psychological distress, exhibiting paranoia and severe anxiety. The clinician is certain that the client has some form of anxiety disorder. The patient has severe liver disease, but the clinician can't determine whether this is a factor; it's possible that the problem is related to other factors such as the client's persistent substance abuse. The most likely DSM-IV diagnosis would be Anxiety Disorder,

    A. provisional
    B. not otherwise specified
    C. with generalized anxiety
    D. undifferentiated

65. Which of the following is NOT generally a guideline for supervisors to follow regarding case presentation?

    A. The presentation should be organized around questions to be answered.
    B. The supervisor should present a case first.
    C. The presentation should progress from practitioner dynamics to client dynamics.
    D. The presentation should be based on written or audiovisual material.

66. A thirty-five-year-old client was referred by a friend because of her sadness and talk of suicide, which were brought on by the death of her lover several years ago but never fully subsided. A practitioner working from the existential viewpoint would view the goal of assessment with this client as

    A. an in-depth understanding of her subjective experience
    B. identifying the support resources already available to her
    C. the identification of situations and stimuli that reinforce her depressive responses
    D. achieving transference

67. Which of the following processes typically occurs LATEST in the therapeutic relationship?

    A. Individuation
    B. Idealization

C. Individualization
D. Identification

68. A social worker has been seeing a client who whose wife left him and moved out of state with the children. During a session, the client says he wishes he could find out where she lives, so he could make her pay for what she's done. The social worker should

    A. call domestic violence experts and document the statement
    B. call domestic violence experts and get legal advice
    C. call the police
    D. try to find the ex-wife and warn her

68.____

69. Some Marxist-oriented behavioral theorists believe that when individuals meet in face-to-face encounters, they make several different adaptations. For example, when individuals of different classes meet, the interaction tends to be very narrow and role-prescribed. This is an example of _____ generalization.

    A. means-end
    B. feelings
    C. control-purposiveness
    D. detachment

69.____

70. A practitioner using rational-emotive therapy to help a child who is depressed has gathered information from the child's parents and teachers, and has collected formal assessment instruments that were completed by the parents and the child. The practitioner then meets with the parents and the child together, and asks the parents a series of questions about their child's symptoms and their history of attempts to deal with the problem. The practitioner's NEXT step should be to

    A. question both the parents and the child about treatment goals
    B. assess the parents and the child for secondary disturbance
    C. ask for the child's opinion of her parents' statements
    D. assess the practical and/or emotional problems presented

70.____

71. The record-keeping requirements at a typical social services agency require the completion of progress notes at an interval no longer than

    A. after every client contact
    B. weekly
    C. every 30 days
    D. every 90 days

71.____

72. NASW policy regarding foster care and transracial adoption states that placement decisions should reflect a child's need for

    A. basic material comforts
    B. continuity
    C. ethnic/racial integrity
    D. a stimulating, challenging environment

72.____

73. Which of the following statements about the behavioral approach to treatment is FALSE?

73.____

A. Behavioral interventions are intended to modify only certain, limited aspects of human behavior
B. Under certain conditions, behaviorists are concerned with affect and cognitions
C. Behaviorists prefer observation over introspection
D. Behaviorists believe that a client's symptoms are merely observable behaviors that have been labeled as problematic

74. Within the family life-cycle perspective, divorces are sometimes referred to as   74.____

    A. derailments
    B. dislocations
    C. non-normative crises
    D. ruptures

75. Which of the following statements is TRUE regarding summative program evaluations?   75.____

    A. Interpretive approaches using qualitative data are particularly useful.
    B. They make no attempt to determine causality.
    C. Validity is a central concern.
    D. Evaluations provide detail about a program's strengths and weaknesses.

KEY (CORRECT ANSWERS)

1. A	16. C	31. D	46. B	61. C
2. A	17. B	32. C	47. D	62. D
3. C	18. A	33. A	48. A	63. B
4. A	19. B	34. B	49. B	64. B
5. B	20. B	35. D	50. C	65. C
6. C	21. A	36. C	51. A	66. A
7. D	22. A	37. D	52. B	67. A
8. A	23. A	38. C	53. C	68. B
9. D	24. D	39. A	54. B	69. A
10. D	25. C	40. C	55. D	70. C
11. A	26. C	41. A	56. B	71. C
12. A	27. B	42. D	57. B	72. B
13. C	28. C	43. C	58. A	73. A
14. C	29. C	44. A	59. A	74. B
15. D	30. C	45. A	60. D	75. C

EXAMINATION SECTION
TEST 1

DIRECTIONS: Each question or incomplete statement is followed by several suggested answers or completions. Select the one that BEST answers the question or completes the statement. *PRINT THE LETTER OF THE CORRECT ANSWER IN THE SPACE AT THE RIGHT.*

1. A breach of ethical conduct may exist when a social worker: 1.____
   - A. discusses sports scores with a client during a session
   - B. uses the client's first name
   - C. exchanges books to be read for pleasure with a client
   - D. exchanges social work sessions for babysitting services by the client

2. A seven-year-old child frequently expresses worry about his parents' whereabouts, is afraid of the dark, cries easily, and complains of frequent stomachaches. The child is MOST likely exhibiting: 2.____
   - A. symptoms of abuse and neglect
   - B. separation anxiety disorder
   - C. conduct disorder
   - D. panic disorder

3. Using behavior therapy for treatment of depression reflects the view that depression is the result of: 3.____
   - A. role confusion
   - B. negative cognition
   - C. poor interpersonal skills
   - D. absence of positive reinforcement

4. A client, referred by his wife, walked into the social worker's office, talking in a loud and threatening manner. He stated that there is no problem except his wife and it is she who should be in therapy. The social worker should FIRST: 4.____
   - A. assure the client that he will have the opportunity to discuss his situation
   - B. suggest to the client that his behavior indicates that he has a problem
   - C. instruct the client to leave the office until he is better composed
   - D. ask the client why he believes his wife needs treatment

5. Which of the following characteristics is usually NOT found in families in which incestuous relationships have occurred?   5.____
   - A. Enmeshment of family members
   - B. Distorted patterns of communication
   - C. Symbiotic mother-child relationships
   - D. Moralistic attitude toward extramarital affairs

6. Following the resignation of a colleague and the freezing of the colleague's position, social work employees of a non-profit agency confronted the social work administrator. They said they were worried about the financial health of the agency and their job security. In addition they complained about the financial disadvantage they experienced in working for the agency. The administrator agreed to a special meeting designed to address employee issues. When planning how to present budgetary issues in a way that would ensure client care, the administrator should focus on: 6.____

A. acknowledging the legitimacy of employees' concerns
B. explaining the fiscal environment of non-profit organizations
C. charging a committee to develop an alternative budget
D. eliciting input about programs needing priority resource allocation

7. A 28-year-old client with a long-standing history of drug use was referred by a concerned relative to a social worker. In the assessment interview, the client tells the social worker about frequent cocaine use. The social worker should FIRST:

    A. conduct a family interview to gather a comprehensive biopsychosocial history
    B. begin psychotherapy focusing on the reason for drug abuse
    C. refer the client for substance abuse treatment as a prerequisite to individual therapy
    D. evaluate the client's motivation for change

8. A family came to a social worker because of their 11-year-old daughter's behavior in the family. The daughter is an average student and has a group of good friends. Within the family, however, she barely speaks to her parents, refuses to clean her room, and rarely brings her friends home. In describing the daughter's behavior, the parents contradict each other, argue about the severity of the behavior, and disagree on methods of discipline. Using a family therapy approach, the social worker should:

    A. focus on the interpersonal communication within the family
    B. offer the parents the chance to work on the marital relationship
    C. help the daughter to function in the family
    D. involve school personnel with the family to determine the extent of the daughter's behavior

9. A social worker saw an unemployed client whose fee was paid by a concerned family member. As a result of effective treatment, the client resumed employment. Part of the benefit package included HMO coverage for behavioral health care. The client wanted to use this mental health benefit to continue with the social worker, who was already a member of the proper provider panel. To make it possible for the client to use the coverage, the social worker should FIRST:

    A. direct the client to obtain a referral from the primary physician
    B. explain the necessity of formalizing a psychiatric diagnosis
    C. seek pre-authorization for sessions before seeing the client again
    D. inform the client that a case manager controls the number of available sessions

10. A client in her late 20s tells her social worker that she "can't stand" the way she looks, saying that she is overweight and unable to use makeup well, and that she appears sloppy and unkempt, and has little fashion sense. She ends by saying "It's overwhelming to even think about how to change." The social worker should FIRST:

    A. teach the client stress reduction techniques
    B. focus on the clients strengths and skills
    C. establish specific behavioral objectives
    D. work with the client to prioritize her concerns

11. The MOST influential factor in determining the probable success of treatment by a social worker whose client is of a different racial background from that of the social worker is the:

    A. social worker's ability to identify with the client
    B. client's transference toward the social worker
    C. social worker's awareness of self
    D. client's ability to communicate openly with the social worker

12. A couple are being seen jointly for problems "with talking to each other." The husband tells the social worker that his wife was sexually abused as a child and he thinks she still has issues with that. The wife confirms the abuse, but denies that it has any relevance to their marital problems, saying she has dealt with the abuse. The husband continues to focus on this topic even after his wife repeatedly asks him to stop. When she yells at him to "just shut up," he does so and turns away from her. She becomes tense and silent. The social worker's MOST appropriate intervention is to:

    A. suggest that the wife and husband be seen individually
    B. suggest they find a topic on which they have less conflict
    C. recommend that they attend a marriage encounter weekend
    D. process with them the observed communication pattern

13. Which of the following statements is true of BOTH supervision and consultation in social work?

    A. The focus is on a continual process of resolving problems identified by the consultant or supervisor.
    B. The level of responsibility of the consultant and supervisor are the same.
    C. The final decision-making authority rests with the consultant or supervisor.
    D. The consultant or the supervisor focus on helping the social worker deal more effectively with problems or tasks.

14. A social worker asks a young child during an assessment interview, "If I asked your parents what they think about you, what would they say?" The social worker is assessing the child's:

    A. dependence on parents   B. reality testing
    C. conscience   D. self-concept

15. The use of silence by a social worker during a session with a client who is expressing a high degree of emotion will be MOST effective in:

    A. demonstrating empathy with the client
    B. relieving the client's tension
    C. developing better rapport with the client
    D. assuring the client that the social worker is listening

16. An adolescent boy in a coeducational inpatient group conducted by a social worker is about to be discharged. The treatment staff recommends that the boy be referred to a group home placement rather than returning home to a chaotic family situation. The group members identify with the boy's feelings of wanting to go home and become furious with the staff for its recommendation. In a group session, they become angry and verbally abuse the social worker. The social worker should FIRST:

    A. explain that the reason the boy should go to the group home is due to the family's instability
    B. explore with the group past negative experiences with group homes
    C. explain to the group that some of the material is confidential because it regards the boy's family and it should not be discussed
    D. acknowledge the group's anger and help members identify the underlying issues

17. Family therapy is contraindicated when:

    A. family members are grossly deceitful and destructive to one another
    B. there is evidence of consistent violation of generational boundaries
    C. family myths and secrets appear to be the family style
    D. the identified client is resistant and unmotivated toward change

18. In establishing a therapeutic relationship with an adult client, the social worker should focus attention on the interpersonal process during:

    A. the initial phase of treatment
    B. the establishment of goals
    C. each phase of treatment
    D. the implementation of goals

19. The major difference between process and outcome evaluation in social work practice is:

    A. outcome evaluation is limited to objective measures; process evaluation involves subjective measures
    B. process evaluation focuses on what was done to achieve results; outcome evaluation is focused on the results
    C. outcome evaluation can be conducted only during the termination stage; process evaluation begins with the assessment stage
    D. data for outcome evaluation is secured from the client; the source for process evaluation data is the social worker

20. During a utilization review phone call, a social worker is asked by the managed care representative to provide specific details of the sexual abuse incidents the client experienced. The social worker should:

    A. provide all requested information to the reviewer
    B. refuse to give specific information to protect the client's privacy
    C. review the release of information with the client prior to providing information
    D. review the managed care contract with the supervisor prior to providing information

21. After careful exploration in psychotherapy regarding mounting anxiety and fear of loss of impulse control, a client decided to seek inpatient admission on a voluntary basis. The social worker arranged for a psychiatric evaluation by a provider approved by the client's managed care insurance company. The psychiatrist refused to support admission and prescribed medication, stating the patient could be stabilized and maintained in the community with appropriate therapy. To help the client understand what happened, the social worker should:

    A. validate the client's plan and send the client for a second opinion
    B. explain the requirements of medical necessity and levels of care
    C. explore the possibility of the client paying for inpatient care
    D. mobilize family members to provide the protection needed by the client

22. In working with adult survivors of childhood sexual abuse, the MOST frequently encountered defense mechanism is:

    A. denial
    B. intellectualization
    C. suppression
    D. projection

23. A client is being seen for an initial session by a social worker in private practice. While discussing her history, the client mentions that she has been hospitalized several times for "depression." When the social worker attempts to explore the hospitalizations, the client become tense and guarded, saying it is "old history." She also declares that she won't give permission for those records to be released. The social worker should FIRST:

    A. explore with the client why this topic appears to be upsetting to her
    B. acknowledge the client's right to decide about release of her records
    C. reassure the client that the focus will be on present issues and concerns
    D. assess the client's current level of depression

24. A social worker who tends to be directive and focused on the client's presenting problem is using which of the following therapeutic models?

    A. Object relations
    B. Cognitive behavioral
    C. Psychoanalytic
    D. Existential

25. A hospital social worker is helping a family plan for the home convalescence of a nine-year-old girl injured in an automobile accident. The family reports difficulty with the school district in arranging for a home teacher. When the social worker attempts to contact the administrator responsible for home teacher assignments, the phone calls are not returned. With the child's discharge one week away, the social worker should FIRST:

    A. contact the superintendent of schools about the urgent need for action
    B. request that the primary physician contact the superintendent of schools
    C. send a registered letter to the administrator with the physician's recommendation for a home teacher
    D. arrange follow-up services with the public health nurse who will provide convalescent care

KEY (CORRECT ANSWERS)

1.	D	11.	C
2.	B	12.	D
3.	D	13.	D
4.	A	14.	D
5.	C	15.	B
6.	D	16.	D
7.	C	17.	A
8.	A	18.	C
9.	A	19.	B
10.	D	20.	C

21. B
22. A
23. B
24. B
25. C

TEST 2

DIRECTIONS: Each question or incomplete statement is followed by several suggested answers or completions. Select the one that BEST answers the question or completes the statement. *PRINT THE LETTER OF THE CORRECT ANSWER IN THE SPACE AT THE RIGHT.*

1. A client whose mother died recently following a long-term illness states to the social worker that he believes that his angry thoughts about his mother caused her death. The client's thoughts are an example of:

    A. delusions
    B. grandiosity
    C. ideas of reference
    D. magical thinking

    1.____

2. Parents of a four-year-old child are referred to a social worker after an examination reveals no physical problem preventing the child from being toilet trained. The parents reveal that the child has not been able to separate from them to attend nursery school, and often sleeps with them even though they have tried to get him to sleep in his own room. During the assessment phase, the social worker's MOST important focus is the:

    A. parents' use of rewards and punishments with the child
    B. early developmental history of each parent
    C. parents' understanding of the child's developmental processes
    D. ways in which the child affects the parents' own relationship

    2.____

3. A 24-year-old woman tells the social worker that she has felt depressed for the past two to three years. She describes herself as feeling sad, with little energy for work or social activities. She also has difficulty making decisions and concentrating on her work, and has a poor appetite. Assessment information does not reveal an apparent reason for the onset of the depressed mood. The client evidences no delusions or hallucinations. According to DSM-IV criteria, the MOST likely diagnosis for the client is:

    A. dysthymic disorder
    B. bipolar disorder, depressed
    C. cyclothymic disorder
    D. major depressive episode, recurrent

    3.____

4. An individual who believes, despite evidence to the contrary, that feelings, thoughts or actions are imposed by an external source, is suffering from:

    A. delirium
    B. delusion
    C. dissociation
    D. dysphoria

    4.____

5. Which of the following medications is used primarily for the treatment of psychosis?

    A. Haloperidol (Haldol)
    B. Alprazolam (Xanax)
    C. Bupropion (Wellbutrin)
    D. Fluoxetine hydrochloride (Prozac)

    5.____

6. A client manifests the characteristics of the early stages of Alzheimer's Disease. To help the client with the changes in her behavior, the MOST appropriate treatment approach for the social worker to use is to focus on:

   A. an understanding of the client's past behavior to enable her to project her future behavior
   B. providing her family members with a support group of other families with similar problems
   C. treatment sessions structured around whatever the client wishes to discuss
   D. observing the progression of the illness and supporting the client in accepting her losses

7. A new client tearfully reports to the social worker that her father, with whom she is very close, is terminally ill. The client's mother, described by her as "very dependent," has already been calling frequently for support and reassurance. The client says "I just don't know how to cope with dad's illness, my mother's demands and my family's needs," and begins to sob. The social worker should FIRST:

   A. acknowledge the client's feelings of being overwhelmed and sad
   B. discuss a referral for hospice care for the father
   C. identify the client's social and family support network
   D. begin exploring ways the client can set limits for her mother

8. A social worker is seeing a lesbian client who is experiencing feelings of frustration, depression, and sadness related to her inability to conceive a child after unsuccessful treatment for infertility problems. She and her partner are considering adoption, but have been rejected by a local agency because of their same gender relationship. The client feels helpless, and does not think she will be successful in fighting the agency bias against same-gender couples. In assisting the client to formulate goals for intervention, the social worker should:

   A. explore the client's motivation to pursue adoption at this time
   B. evaluate where the client is in her coming-out process
   C. help the client to confront the discriminatory policies of the agency
   D. refer the client for medication evaluation for depression

9. A client is complaining about her friend, stating that she is selfish and insensitive. The social worker asks if this is the same friend whom the client had described the week before as caring and a true friend. The client confirms that it is the same person. The social worker comments that this is a complete change in the client's way of thinking. The social worker is using the intervention of:

   A. Interpretation
   B. Reality testing
   C. Confrontation
   D. Clarification

10. Which of the following actions by a social worker is considered unethical?

    A. Receiving a fee for the referral of a client to another practitioner
    B. Informing the client of fees in advance of services
    C. Engaging in private practice while holding an agency employment
    D. Establishing rates for professional services not commensurate with that of other professionals

11. A social worker, many of whose clients are in crisis, carries a heavy and difficult case load. In discussing the cases with the supervisor, the social worker reports that clients "come in with a laundry list of complaints" and efforts to help them resolve their problems result in the social worker feeling angry and frustrated or distant and bored. The social worker is MOST likely dealing with the issue of:

    A. transference
    B. countertransference
    C. job-related stress
    D. depression

12. When authorization for treatment from a managed care company is requested, the PRIMARY determinant for approval is based upon:

    A. treatment goals that are explicit and measurable
    B. a diagnosis covered by the insurance plan
    C. documentation that medical necessity criteria are met
    D. a treatment plan providing the least restrictive level of care

13. After six marital therapy sessions with a social worker, a couple continued their destructive pattern of fighting. During the next session, the couple began yelling at each other in a loud and threatening manner. The social worker stopped them and stated, "Your situation is hopeless; fight as often as you wish." This technique is known as:

    A. encouragement
    B. reframing
    C. prescribing a ritual
    D. paradoxical directive

14. According to ego psychology, projective identification is a concept that describes the process of:

    A. unconsciously perceiving others' behavior as a reflection of one's own attitudes
    B. consciously imitating the characteristics of a significant other
    C. showing another person how to develop a better self-image through modeling
    D. associating characteristics from a significant person in the past with another in the present

15. The executive director in an expanding nonprofit social service agency increasingly involved the Director of Professional Services (DPS) in overall agency planning and decision-making. To participate and still perform DPS functions, this manager delegated some activities to senior professionals. According to principles of delegation, the DPS could shift:

    A. responsibility for task completion
    B. authority to perform tasks
    C. power and influence
    D. responsibility for managerial decisions

16. In interviewing a client, a social worker seeks concreteness from the client for all of the following purposes EXCEPT to:

    A. avoid emotionally charged topics
    B. elicit the client's specific feelings
    C. clarify a client message
    D. focus on the "here and now"

17. In planning to evaluate social work treatment in an agency, the MOST important consideration is:

    A. the amount of clinical staff time the evaluation will require
    B. whether the results of the evaluation can be applied to other services
    C. information the evaluation will yield for treatment decision-making
    D. involvement of clinical staff in the planning of the evaluation strategy

18. A couple in their mid-50s came to a family agency accompanied by their adult daughter who lives in their home. They describe marital difficulties which began after the husband suffered a mild stroke. The wife said that he has frequent outbursts of anger, has lost interest in his personal care, and is fearful of being left alone. The husband stated that his wife is overprotective of him, and described the daughter as "nervous when I try to do anything for myself." Using a structural family therapy approach, the social worker would focus on:

    A. obtaining a complete history of the marital and family relationships
    B. creating a situation in the interview which would place the husband in a dependent role
    C. exploring with all family members their feelings about the effects of the stroke on family relationships
    D. arranging individual treatment sessions for each family member

19. A social worker used three different techniques with a depressed client, introducing each of the treatment techniques in order over a period of time. To compare the effectiveness of each of the techniques in helping the client reach the treatment goal, which of the following designs should the social worker use?

    A. A-B design
    B. Multiple baseline across behaviors design
    C. A-B-A-B design
    D. Within-series design

20. An adult who has come to a hospital emergency room complains of visual hallucinations, confusion, and restlessness. Physical symptoms include chills, dilated pupils, and nausea. When interviewed by the social worker, the client states, "Nothing is wrong; I just need some sleep. Which of the following substances is MOST likely the cause of the client's condition?

    A. Alcohol
    B. Marijuana
    C. Cocaine
    D. Barbiturates

21. After several sessions in individual treatment with a social worker, a married woman client reveals that she has had an ongoing affair during the last five years. She says that she is unhappy in her marriage but wants to remain with her husband until her children are in college. She believes her husband does not suspect her

infidelity but is often upset that she does not spend enough time with him. The BEST plan for the social worker in this situation is to:

    A. focus the treatment on the client's feelings about the situation
    B. schedule sessions with the entire family
    C. see the couple together
    D. refer the husband to another therapist

22. A social worker has been appointed to the board of directors of a family counseling agency. All of the following are appropriate actions for the social worker as a board member EXCEPT:

    A. determining the performance criteria for the agency director position
    B. reviewing data about utilization of agency services by clients
    C. acting as a paid consultant to agency staff who deliver direct services
    D. serving as chair of a board committee on service delivery

23. For the fifth session with a social worker, a client arrived ten minutes late. Upon entering the social worker's office, the client remained standing and said in an anxious tone, "I know I'm late, but I had other things to do, I just couldn't leave work today." The social worker's BEST response would be to say:

    A. "You seem to think more of your work than you do of coming here."
    B. "Maybe we need to explore what it means to you to come here for our sessions."
    C. "I know that your work is important, but my time is valuable. We will just have less time together today."
    D. "You seem to think that I would be angry with you for being late today. Let's talk about what you anticipated I would say."

24. When reviewing a social worker's performance, the supervisor recognized that the social worker conveyed little empathy toward clients who had recently left welfare and were holding first jobs. In order to help the social worker increase the number of empathetically accurate statements made to clients, the supervisor should:

    A. explain welfare-to-work procedures from the client's perspective
    B. suggest that the social worker enter therapy to become a more empathic person
    C. model empathic communication when engaging with the worker
    D. assert clearly the agency's commitment to supporting these clients

25. Borderline personality disorder is characterized by all of the following characteristics EXCEPT:
    A. intense long-term relationships   B. primitive delusional fantasies
    C. lack of control of aggressive drives   D. self-destructive behavior

KEY (CORRECT ANSWERS)

1. D
2. C
3. A
4. B
5. A

6. D
7. A
8. C
9. C
10. A

11. B
12. C
13. D
14. A
15. B

16. A
17. C
18. B
19. D
20. C

21. A
22. C
23. D
24. C
25. A

EXAMINATION SECTION
TEST 1

DIRECTIONS: Each question or incomplete statement is followed by several suggested answers or completions. Select the one the BEST answers the question or completes the statement. *PRINT THE LETTER OF THE CORRECT ANSWER IN THE SPACE AT THE RIGHT.*

1. A client and a professional meet to discuss the client's drinking problem and how it relates to the problems she's having in putting her life back together after leaving her abusive husband. During the interview, the worker asks the client: "You would be in a better position to hold down a job if you stopped drinking, wouldn't you?" This question will signal to the client that the professional

    A. is more worried about whether the client can support herself than about whether she can stop drinking
    B. is not really asking a question, but already has an answer in mind
    C. does not understand the difficulties involved in alcoholism
    D. cares about whether the client remains employed

2. Typically—and unless the client is in crisis—the questioning process in a helping interview should progress

    A. chronologically
    B. from general to specific
    C. from specific to general
    D. in a series of grouped topical units

3. When interviewing a client, a professional may sometimes make use of the questioning technique known as the "reaction probe." The purpose of the technique is to

    A. point out inadequately covered content
    B. increase the emotional depth of the interview
    C. provoke an affective reaction from the client
    D. elicit a clearer explanation of personal situations

4. Of the following techniques or strategies that can be used by a professional during a client interview, which is most directive in nature?

    A. Clarifying
    B. Reflecting
    C. Interpretation
    D. Paraphrasing

5. The primary effect of confrontation during a client interview is to

    A. break down client defenses
    B. initiate reconsideration of behaviors
    C. force a client to face the facts
    D. introduce unpleasant content

6. During an interview with a battered young woman, the victim reaches the conclusion that she would like to return home. The professional has met with this woman several times previously, and has a strong personal feeling that she should leave the abusive situation. The BEST move on the part of the professional at this point would be to

   A. try to help the client clarify the reasons behind her decision
   B. advise the client that her life may be in danger if she stays in this situation
   C. say nothing and leave the woman to make her own decisions
   D. tell the client that a room has been reserved for her at a local shelter, and that she should stay there for a while

7. During an interview, a professional sometimes utters minimal encouragements ("uh-huh," "I see," "hmm") while a client is speaking. Usually, the effect of these essentially meaningless sounds is to

   A. distract the client from what she is trying to say
   B. assure the client that the professional is present and involved
   C. give the impression that the professinoal is only pretending to listen
   D. steer the client toward a particular topic or area of interest

8. During an interview with a client who has proven somewhat resistant the professional encounters a long silence from the client, who has just cut herself off in mid-sentence and is staring at the worker. The FIRST thing the worker should try to break the silence is to

   A. summarize the client's last thoughts
   B. say something such as "uh-huh" or "I see," and then wait a moment
   C. say, "I wonder why you're silent."
   D. wait patiently for at least a minute before interjecting

9. During a client interview, the listening/intervention technique known as "reflection of feeling" is used to

   A. intensify the depth of the interview
   B. encourage specific content for discussion
   C. respond to the client's verbalize thinking
   D. bring essential content to the surface of the discussion

10. During the assessment phase of an interview, checklists are most useful for identifying and selecting

    A. problems for intervention
    B. specific objectives
    C. available resources
    D. general goals

11. Of the following, which should probably take place FIRST during an intake interview?

    A. Developmental history
    B. Statement of presenting problem
    C. Initial intervention
    D. Cross-sectional history

12. In using the "reflection of meaning" technique in a client interview, a professional should do each of the following, EXCEPT

    A. begin with a sentence stem such as "You mean..." or "Sounds like you believe..."
    B. offer an interpretation of the client's words.
    C. add paraphrasing of longer client statements.
    D. close with a "check-out" such as, "Am I hearing you right?"

13. In which of the following situations is the use of "small talk" in an opening interview MOST likely to be contraindicated?

    A. Referral for ongoing marital problems
    B. Home visit to a general assistance client
    C. Domestic crisis intervention
    D. Court-ordered anger management counseling

14. During an interview with a family, a professional observes that the youngest son often exhibits overly adaptive behavior – he strenuously attempts to comfort the father when the father appears to be upset. Later, the practitioner learns that in school, the child often becomes uneasy or upset whenever another child cries or acts out. The practitioner should interpret these signs as suggestive of possible

    A. repressed memories of past trauma
    B. sexual abuse
    C. formation of a dysfunctional triad
    D. physical abuse

15. During an assessment interview, a professional and client explore the range of problems that most concern the client. The NEXT step for the professional and client would be to

    A. rank the problems in their priority to the client
    B. determine how progress will be measured as these problems are addressed
    C. identify barriers to resolving each problem
    D. define each problem in explicit behavioral terms

16. When an interviewer considers what type of nonverbal behavior will be appropriate given the interviewee's cultural background, the interviewer is making a decision about

    A. processing
    B. encoding
    C. decoding
    D. transmission

17. Questions that begin with the word "_____" are typically theones that clients find most frustrating to answer in an interview.

    A. have
    B. why
    C. what
    D. how

18. During an interview, a client expresses feelings of being different or deviant. Which of the following techniques would be MOST appropriate for counteracting these feelings?

    A. Encouragement
    B. Reassurance
    C. Negative reinforcement
    D. Universalization

19. During an assessment interview, a husband who has been convicted of physically abusing his wife states that the reason for the abuse was because "that's all she understands." In this case, the husband is practicing

    A. rationalization
    B. intellectualization
    C. a task-focused coping strategy
    D. an emotion-focused coping strategy

20. Accommodating is a skill in which domestic violence professionals communicate to the clients that they are being heard. This technique also assists professionals by ensuring that they have a clear understanding of the client's perceptions of the problems. Accommodating skills consist of
    I. attending behaviors
    II. concreteness
    III. reflections
    IV. tracking

    A. I only
    B. I, II and III
    C. II and III
    D. I, II, III and IV

21. During an assessment interview, a professional and a client try to clarify and analyze the client's sense of self. If the worker wants to discover something about the client's self-acceptance, which of the following questions is MOST appropriate?

    A. To what extent do you worry about illness and physical incapacity?
    B. Is what you expect to happen mostly good or mostly bad?
    C. Do you enjoy the times when you are alone?
    D. Where do your other family members live?

22. Concreteness assists clients in focusing conversation or messages from vagueness to descriptive, specific, and operational language. Vagueness is often used unconsciously by clients to avoid addressing painful issues. Domestic professionals have the responsibility to assist clients in making concrete statements. Concreteness can be encouraged by:
    I. examining perceptions and exploring the basis for the client's conclusions
    II. using concrete responses with clients
    III. clarifying unspecific or unfamiliar terms
    IV. drawing out details about experiences, interactions and behaviors

    A. I and II
    B. I, II and III

C. II and III
D. I, II, III and IV

23. Each of the following is a general guideline that should be used for effective listening during the interview process, EXCEPT

    A. have a clear idea of the purpose of the interview before the session begins
    B. assume and accept a certain level of ignorance on the part of oneself
    C. develop a clear expectation about what the client will say during the interview
    D. listen for recurrent and dominant themes, rather than focus on detail

23.____

24. When interacting with clients from different cultures, domestic violence professionals must

    I. recognize that discrepancies about time can be legitimate cultural differences
    II. address clients as Mr., Ms., or Mrs. until given permission to use first names
    III. recognize that handshakes are intimate in some cultures and casual in others
    IV. be mindful that different cultures may assign different levels of authority and formality to the helping relationship

    A. I and II
    B. II only
    C. II, III and IV
    D. I, II, III and IV

24.____

25. During a client interview, a professional often repeats verbatim a key word or phrase from the client's last response. The purpose of this repetition of content is to

    A. confront the client with contradictions or inaccuracies in his/her statements
    B. open the door for an interpretation of the client's statement
    C. encourage the client's choice of material to pursue
    D. distill client statements to their essential components

25.____

KEY (CORRECT ANSWERS)

1. B
2. B
3. B
4. C
5. B

6. A
7. B
8. B
9. A
10. D

11. B
12. B
13. C
14. D
15. D

16. B
17. B
18. D
19. A
20. B

21. C
22. D
23. C
24. D
25. C

TEST 2

DIRECTIONS: Each question or incomplete statement is followed by several suggested answers or completions. Select the one the BEST answers the question or completes the statement. *PRINT THE LETTER OF THE CORRECT ANSWER IN THE SPACE AT THE RIGHT.*

1. Helping professionals often make use of reframing to influence the direction of interviews. In the case of domestic violence, professionals should exercise extreme caution with this technique–if used improperly, it could

    A. suggest to the client that there is some positive intent behind the abuser's behavior
    B. alter the direction of information-gathering, from specific to general
    C. create a kind of victim/rescuer relationship between the client and the professional
    D. make the client to believe that he/she is not really being abused

2. In client interviews, "psychological attending" refers to how professionals

    A. congruently respond to the observed verbal and nonverbal behaviors of clients
    B. restate behaviors or beliefs in more positive ways
    C. convey a non-judgemental attitude
    D. restate of the person's multiple statements of feeling or content expressed over time

3. Tracking consists of a set of techniques that allows domestic violence professionals to influence the direction of interviews. Tracking skills include each of the following, EXCEPT

    A. summarization
    B. questions
    C. positive reframing
    D. springboarding

4. Which of the following questions or statements is MOST appropriate for a professional in initiating a helping relationship?

    A. "I understand you have a problem."
    B. "You came in here to see me about _____."
    C. "How can I help you today?"
    D. "I'm glad you came in to see me."

5. Which of the following is a guideline that should be observed in developing an assessment questionnaire for domestic violence victims?

    A. Develop several focused questionnaires rather than one all-purpose one.
    B. The most sensitive or probing questions should appear near the middle of the questionnaire.
    C. For complex ideas, form two-part questions.
    D. Include only open-ended questions.

6. General guidelines for cross-cultural interviews include
    I. the use of summarizing in interviews
    II. focusing on closed rather than open questions
    III. remembering that not all cultures value openness and authenticity
    IV. extensive use of self-disclosure to increase client comfort

    A. I only
    B. I and II
    C. II, III and IV
    D. I, II, III and IV

7. In general, it is believed that interviewers who spend less than a minimum of _____ of an interview listening to the client are moreactive than they should be.

    A. one-fourth
    B. one-third
    C. one-half
    D. two thirds

8. In comparing a normal conversation and a helping interview, which of the following statements is generally TRUE?

    A. A conversation involves no subsequent accountability.
    B. A conversation involves a clear delineation of roles.
    C. An interview involves an equal distribution of power and authority.
    D. The interaction in an interview follows social expectations and norms.

9. In a client interview, a worker should typically use self-disclosure

    A. at a level that is tailored to client feedback
    B. intensely during the treatment phase in order to establish a bond
    C. as early as possible in the process to establish the expectation
    D. before other methods at client revelation have been attempted

10. During an intake interview, a professional makes the decision to severely curtail the gathering of past history between the client and her abuser, and instead focus on current interactions. Probably the greatest risk involved in this approach is that

    A. the heightened sense of emotional involvement might overwhelm the client
    B. the client may begin to doubt the competency of the therapist
    C. the client may become confused about the therapist's purpose
    D. there may be a lower degree of authenticity in client interactions

11. During an assessment interview, a professional should try as much as possible to get a client to arrange her description of the presenting problem

    A. narratively, in terms of how she sees it, no matter how incoherent
    B. chronologically, to facilitate the composition of a sociohistory
    C. thematically, in terms of recurring issues and problems in her life
    D. empirically, in terms only of what happened on particular dates or during particular periods

12. Which of the following is a guideline that should be used regarding the use of interpretation during a client interview?

    A. If a client rejects the interpretation, be prepared to defend it.
    B. Interpretations are most useful during intake and assessment interviews.
    C. Interpretations must be offered immediately after the statement that provokes them.
    D. Offer interpretations tentatively, as a hypothesis.

13. Which of the following is a disadvantage associated with the use of closed questions in client interviews?

    A. May discourage reluctant or resistant clients from participating
    B. More difficult format for less experienced interviewers
    C. May encourage passive and restricted client participation
    D. Risks failure to obtain specific detailed content

14. Interviewing in the helping professions is often divided into four stages. Which of the following is MOST likely to be omitted during early interviews with domestic violence victims?

    A. Social
    B. Problem definition
    C. Focus
    D. Closure

15. Which of the following is NOT a guideline that should be used by a professional in summarizing during an interview?

    A. Summarize when a transition to new content is desirable.
    B. The content of summaries should be ordered in the same way that the client ordered it, in order to avoid confusion.
    C. Wait to summarize until the content is sufficient to suggest a general theme.
    D. The client should participate in summarizing, either by summarizing him/herself, or by responding to the worker's summary.

16. In the helping interview, "facilitative genuineness" refers to

    A. an absence of mixed messages in communication with a person to affect change
    B. conveying the appropriate amount of authority for inspiring faith in the client
    C. tuning into a person's emotions and communicating understanding without losing objectivity
    D. the ability to maintain a non-judgmental attitude that conveys caring, concern, and acceptance of the other person as a unique human being

17. Which of the following should typically NOT be an objective of a worker's self-disclosure during a client interview?

    A. Facilitating the client's willingness to communicate
    B. Modeling appropriate behavior for the client
    C. Pointing out an appropriate resolution or course of action
    D. Provoking a catharsis for the client

18. Usually, the purpose of opening an initial client interview with general conversation or "small talk" is to

    A. construct an unobtrusive opportunity for making and recording initial observations
    B. ease the client's transition from a familiar mode of speaking into a new and unfamiliar role
    C. soften the client's defenses so that initial questioning will catch him/ her off guard
    D. downplay the seriousness of the interview

18.____

19. In client interviews, supportive statements by the professional are MOST likely to be effective if he or she can

    A. set aside feelings of disapproval for other client behaviors
    B. identify the client's feeling or the behavior for which the practitioner is expressing approval or encouragement
    C. use the statement to steer the client toward a specific course of action
    D. differentiate between the times when a client is genuinely hurting and when he/she is simply trying to gain sympathy

19.____

20. During a conversation, the wife of an abuser says to a domestic violence professional: "I just don't feel as if I have any friends out there who can help me deal with this".
    The domestic violence professional responds by saying: "It's important to you to have friends who help you through tough times".
    "Yes," the client says.
    The professional says: "Was there a time when you did - when there were friends you could turn to?"
    In this conversation, the professional is making use of the techniques

    A. reflecting and summarizing
    B. refraining and springboarding
    C. clarifying and attending
    D. problem definition and closure

20.____

21. Typically, the _____ stage of an interview is the one which ismost powerful in determining the interviewee's impression of the interview as a whole.

    A. opening
    B. questioning
    C. closing
    D. discussion

21.____

22. During an interview with a client, the professional says: "You remember a while ago, when we were talking about your wedding, you mentioned that that was the greatest day of your life. Can you tell me why you felt this way?" This is an example of the technique known as _____ transition.

    A. mutational
    B. cued
    C. reversional
    D. confrontational

22.____

23. During an interview, a client says, "He's changed completely. Sometimes it doesn't seem as if he has any feelings left for me."
The professional responds by saying: "You seem to think he doesn't love you very much".
The client says, "So you think he loves me very much? What makes you say that?"
What has just occurred in this interview could be defined as a

   A. projection
   B. reaction formation
   C. displacement
   D. repression

23.____

24. Advantages of the use of open-ended questions in client interviews include
   I. maximizing client freedom regarding content
   II. providing client's cognitive and affective views of problem
   III. easier format for inexperienced interviewers
   IV. maximizing worker access to desirable data

   A. I and II
   B. I, II and III
   C. III only
   D. I, II, III and IV

24.____

25. During an assessment interview, a client tends to ramble through many digressions in recounting her situation. In order to lend coherence to the session, the BEST approach on the part of the professional would be to

   A. gently interrupting digressions with a reminder of the interview's purpose
   B. offer gentle reminders to the client after she has finished with a digression
   C. occasionally paraphrase client statements
   D. offer periodic summaries of the client's accounts

25.____

KEY (CORRECT ANSWERS)

1. A
2. A
3. A
4. B
5. A

6. A
7. D
8. C
9. A
10. A

11. A
12. D
13. C
14. A
15. B

16. A
17. C
18. B
19. B
20. B

21. C
22. C
23. B
24. A
25. D

EXAMINATION SECTION
TEST 1

DIRECTIONS: Each question or incomplete statement is followed by several suggested answers or completions. Select the one that BEST answers the question or completes the statement. *PRINT THE LETTER OF THE CORRECT ANSWER IN THE SPACE AT THE RIGHT.*

1. A supervisor should consider a social worker to be skilled in diagnosis if, of the following, the worker excels in

    A. categorizing behavior, personality, and social problems in syndrome classes using a standardized nomenclature
    B. relating diagnoses to a theoretical system such as Freudian, Adlerian, Rogerian, etc.
    C. describing the person, problem, and setting as related to the casework situation
    D. determining the genesis of the problems for which the client seeks help

2. The one of the following which is the BASIC difference between the function of a supervisor and the function of a consultant in a large social agency is that the supervisor

    A. is a permanent staff member, while the consultant is a person brought in from the outside
    B. trains young and experienced workers, while the consultant trains those who no longer need supervision
    C. has administrative responsibility for agency operation, while the consultant has no direct administrative responsibility
    D. has a personal relationship with the worker, while the consultant provides administrative controls for evaluating the supervisor

3. Experts in social work supervision have stated that the role of the supervisor should be *authoritative* rather than *authoritarian*.
    Of the following, this means MOST NEARLY that the supervisor's authority should come from

    A. his superior skill and competence
    B. his ability to exercise democratic control
    C. responsibility delegated through administrative channels
    D. differences in role perception of the worker and the supervisor

4. Assume that a supervisor who finds himself immobilized in the face of a difficult problem complains because his subordinates are confused and indecisive.
    Of the following, it is MOST probable that the supervisor

    A. needs to give more guidance to his subordinates so that they will be able to make decisions within their sphere of responsibility
    B. is projecting his own state of mind on to his subordinates and is venting his feelings of frustration on their incompetence
    C. requires professional help for a personality problem which may make him unsuited for supervisory responsibility
    D. should arrange for his subordinates to get special training in decision-making within their areas of responsibility

5. A supervisor in a large agency with a recent graduate of a school of social work on his staff should be aware that the one of the following which is a common problem of the new professional worker is a tendency to

   A. interpret agency rules and regulations literally because of the desire for supervisory approval
   B. feel frustrated because agency rules and regulations prevent him from making independent decisions based on his professional training
   C. make independent decisions without calling upon the supervisor for expert advice and guidance
   D. protect himself from situations of stress by working with his clients in a routine, uninspired manner

6. Assume that your agency has a serious shortage of professional staff. However, an analysis of the daily tasks of professional social workers reveals that many of the tasks performed are of a clerical or administrative nature.
Of the following, the MOST appropriate step to take FIRST in order to alleviate the shortage is to

   A. hire indigenous paraprofessionals from the community to take over part of the job load
   B. assign clerical and administrative staff to take over these non-professional tasks
   C. survey professional social workers in order to determine whether some of these clerical or administrative tasks are superfluous
   D. determine how many additional professional social workers are needed and arrange for recruitment in accordance with requirements

7. Experts have made a distinction between the formal and the informal organization of a large agency.
Of the following, the informal organization has been described as

   A. dysfunctional due to its inevitable conflict with the basic objectives of the agency
   B. those levels of the agency which are separate from the administrative units which have direct responsibility for policy formulation
   C. including only those positions within the agency which have no direct responsibility for its service delivery function
   D. those relationships and channels of communication that resourceful employees develop and use in order to get the work done

8. The term *bureaucracy* has invidious implications for the general public. To the social scientist, however, *bureaucracy* is a technical term for a large, complex organization.
Of the following, according to the social scientist, a *bureaucracy* is structured on rational principles and characterized by

   A. a democratic system in which each person has maximum freedom to make his own decisions
   B. a strict and well-defined hierarchy of authority functioning on the basis of clear-cut chain of command principles
   C. the assignment of independent responsibility to administrative and professional personnel responsible for delivery of services
   D. equal accessibility of all personnel within program units of the agency to personnel at the level where decisions are made

9. In the hierarchical administrative organization which is characteristic of a large agency, levels of authority emanate from the top downward.
   Of the following, this structure has a tendency toward

   A. decreasing opportunities for staff participation in areas beyond their immediately circumscribed responsibilities
   B. easing the communications flow between departmental lines at the lower levels of the hierarchy
   C. permitting the flow of communication from the top downward, but not from the bottom upward
   D. structural flexibility which adapts readily to changing demands upon the organization

10. Of the following, adherence to *democratic* principles in the administration of a large agency means MOST NEARLY

    A. the feeling of all employees that they are participating in planning and policy making
    B. an equal voice for all employees in planning and policy making
    C. relevant participation of all employees according to their special competence
    D. friendliness, regardless of rank, among all employees at all levels

11. The one of the following which is the MOST important reason that all social workers who work in large agencies should be well-oriented to the administrative process is that they will

    A. be better qualified to participate in planning, decision-making, and formulation of policies
    B. be more sensitive to the needs of extra-agency components in the agency administrative system
    C. have a greater capacity to contribute to the agency and to accept their responsibilities within the system of cooperative effort
    D. be qualified for appointment to positions which do not include direct involvement in service

12. By virtue of training and orientation, social workers are well aware of personality traits that enhance or diminish administrative competence. Social agencies are becoming increasingly conscious, however, of the importance of understanding the effects of different forms of agency organization and structure, not only in relation to staff performance but also in relation to the service the agency performs.
    Of the following, this statement means MOST NEARLY that

    A. administrative difficulties can be analyzed and resolved, not only in terms of personality shortcomings of given individuals but also in terms of organizational arrangements
    B. such factors in agency organization as size, physical arrangements, and organizational roles can be more important than personality traits of administrators in influencing effective delivery of services
    C. agency organization and structure can have a significant effect on staff performance
    D. social workers should give more emphasis to the importance of understanding the effects of agency organization and structure, rather than personality traits

13. According to the task-centered concept of administrative organization, attention is focused on the problem or task at hand, involving all persons who may have a contribution to make, regardless of their professional status or rank in the organization.
Of the following, the MOST probable result of such an approach to agency administration would be to

    A. increase delegation of responsibility from the top downward
    B. increase promotion opportunities for non-professionals
    C. enhance the opportunities for staff to participate in policy formulations
    D. interfere with hierarchical distribution of authority from the top downward

14. The one of the following which CORRECTLY describes the change of focus in social work today is:

    A. New psychological studies and research on human behavior have resulted in increased emphasis on personality problems and the need to change individual dependency patterns
    B. The psychoanalytic orientation and the emphasis on personality problems are being challenged by social science perspectives which stress the environmental causes of individual maladjustment
    C. Emphasis on giving clients supportive assistance with personal problems and on changing individual behavior patterns has shifted to heightened attention to decreasing dependency through required work programs
    D. Sociological studies and other research in the social sciences have resulted in a new emphasis on changing family life and substituting communal ways of living for obsolete institutions

15. The one of the following which is an important distinction between the profession of social work and many other professions is that

    A. there is a basic conflict between social workers' professional interests and the interests of the agency in which they are employed
    B. there is little activity by social workers in the direction of private practice
    C. the claim for recognition of social work as a profession arose when it was practiced mainly within administrative organizations
    D. social workers have a tendency to move from private practice to practice within administrative organizations

16. As the supervisor for the After Hours Emergency Child Care Services, you have been asked by a group of home aides whether they could go out in pairs to areas of the city where they feel uneasy and where some of them have had unpleasant experiences. They point out that caseworkers have approval for this although they usually visit these neighborhoods during daytime hours, while home aides are in the field at all hours of the night. Of the following, your BEST response would be to

    A. remind the home aides that they knew the working conditions when they were hired
    B. question the statement that caseworkers have approval to go in the field in pairs
    C. sympathize with the home aides' fears and agree that their work presents many challenges
    D. indicate that you will consider each such request on an individual basis so that all possible protective measures can be taken

17. At a meeting of your supervisory staff, several supervisors inform you that they lack staff to provide coverage for all service requests. Some units are more overburdened than others because some kinds of service requests are more numerous. A group of caseworkers have suggested to their supervisors that all service requests be distributed throughout the units, instead of continuing the present system of sending requests to specialized units.
Of the following, your BEST immediate response to this proposal would be to

    A. indicate that assignment of work is not a decision to be made by casework staff, but that you will forward the suggestion to your supervisor
    B. point out that, although you have made this serious situation known at higher levels, you do not have the authority to reorganize your units in the manner suggested
    C. ask the supervisors to submit more factual data on volume, distribution of cases, and staff available, along with their recommendations as to the feasibility of the caseworkers' proposal
    D. draft a memo to your supervisor stating that staff shortages are now so serious that caseworkers cannot cover all service requests, and ask for instructions

18. An institution or group home is usually the BEST placement for

    A. children who are committed by the court because of neglect or abuse by their parents
    B. adolescents and school-age children who have temporarily lost their ability to relate to parent substitutes
    C. pre-school age children whose parents cannot care for them temporarily
    D. children who have difficulty relating to their peers

19. Foster homes must be periodically re-examined as a requirement for continued licensing. Of the following, the MOST important reason for this requirement is that

    A. homes that have been used for many years tend to deteriorate and may need to be closed
    B. child welfare workers often do not see the foster fathers at any other time
    C. foster parents may become overwhelmed by too many placements and may desire to have their homes closed
    D. changes in the composition and competence of a foster family should be evaluated and reported regularly

20. A child welfare agency can USUALLY expect that new foster parents who have children of their own will

    A. take on the role of foster parents with very little difficulty
    B. need more help than childless couples in adjusting to their new roles
    C. need to have their responsibilities to their foster children clearly differentiated from their responsibilities to their own children
    D. have a good understanding of the needs of foster children and adjust quickly to the agency's role in providing care for them

21. When a young child makes repeated attempts to break through the reasonable limits which his foster parents have set on his behavior, it is PROBABLY a sign that

    A. the foster parents are not punishing him appropriately for his misbehavior
    B. he does not respect parental authority

C. he is testing whether his foster parents care enough about him to discipline him
D. the foster parents should be more lenient with him

22. Adoptive parents should be provided with factual information about the child's natural parents MAINLY

    A. in order to be able to answer his questions about his natural parents
    B. because they would try to obtain this information anyway
    C. so that they can be prevented from worrying about the child's background
    D. to encourage them to tell the child about his natural parents

23. Foster parents are usually responsible for transporting and accompanying their foster children to various appointments arranged by the child welfare worker.
When a foster parent informs the worker that he is unable to keep a specific appointment, the worker should

    A. accompany the child to the appointment himself
    B. insist that the foster parent keep the appointment
    C. reschedule the appointment for a time more convenient for the foster parent
    D. evaluate whether cancellation of the appointment would be harmful, and act accordingly

24. After spending several months in a congregate shelter, John is to be placed in a foster home with his younger siblings. However, the discharge physical reveals that he needs a tonsillectomy.
In this situation, the child welfare worker should FIRST

    A. ask the shelter to arrange for John's tonsillectomy and postpone the placement until after the operation
    B. ask the doctor if he considers the tonsillectomy to be urgent so the worker can decide whether or not to postpone the placement
    C. arrange for the tonsillectomy at once and have John hospitalized
    D. tell the prospective foster mother about the need for the tonsillectomy so she can decide when the surgery should be done

25. An eight-month-old baby, born with withdrawal symptoms and abandoned by her drug-addicted mother, is being made ready for placement in a foster home.
In this situation, the child welfare worker should

    A. not tell the prospective foster parents about the natural mother's drug addiction so that they won't become unduly worried
    B. tell the prospective foster parents about the natural mother's addiction but assure them that the child has been treated and cured
    C. inform the prospective foster parents of the child's background, explain that she may have a convulsion, and tell them what to do if this should happen
    D. not tell the prospective foster parents about the child's background unless they ask

KEY (CORRECT ANSWERS)

1.	C	11.	C
2.	C	12.	A
3.	A	13.	C
4.	B	14.	B
5.	B	15.	C
6.	B	16.	D
7.	D	17.	C
8.	B	18.	B
9.	A	19.	D
10.	C	20.	C

21. C
22. A
23. D
24. B
25. C

TEST 2

DIRECTIONS: Each question or incomplete statement is followed by several suggested answers or completions. Select the one that BEST answers the question or completes the statement. *PRINT THE LETTER OF THE CORRECT ANSWER IN THE SPACE AT THE RIGHT.*

1. Of the following, the BEST placement for a twelve-year-old boy who has been diagnosed as having a severe behavior disorder would probably be in a(n)   1.____

    A. small group home which is programmed to offer a permissive living atmosphere and home instruction from the State Department of Education
    B. institution geared to treat pre-delinquent children
    C. foster home where his acting out behavior would be understood and accepted
    D. institution where his behavior would be controlled through routines, discipline, and relationships with adults and peers

2. In planning services for a young woman expecting an out-of-wedlock child, the child welfare worker should be PRIMARILY concerned with   2.____

    A. obtaining as much information as possible about the young woman's ethnic background and health history
    B. determining how the young woman's family is reacting to the situation and whether they will help plan for the unborn child
    C. making up a list of suitable adoption agencies to which the young woman can be referred
    D. providing the young woman with information about all the various arrangements she can make for her unborn child

3. A foster mother who has been caring for two retarded preschool children, and receiving a special board rate for the foster care, has become very tired. Her doctor has told her that she needs a vacation, and she so informs the child welfare worker. However, she does not wish to give up caring for the children.   3.____
Of the following, the BEST approach for the worker to take is to

    A. recognize the foster mother's need for a vacation and make temporary arrangements for the care of the children
    B. remind the foster mother that she is receiving a special board rate which should be enough to provide her with babysitting relief
    C. find a new facility for the children since the foster mother's health is apparently failing as a result of taking care of the children
    D. try to determine if there is another reason for the foster mother's exhaustion

4. In planning for 18-month-old twins, one who appears to be developing normally and one who is functioning below normal and has many physical problems, the child welfare worker should place the GREATEST emphasis on   4.____

    A. placing them in one foster home since research has shown that a symbiotic relationship exists between twins
    B. placing them separately since it would be psychologically harmful for the *normal* twin to live with his *abnormal* sibling

C. finding an institution that has a specially trained staff for taking care of handicapped children but also accepts *normal* children so that the twins could remain together
D. finding an appropriate placement for each child according to his needs, realizing that meeting their individual needs is more important than their twin-ship

5. A mother has had all five of her children in placement since she was hospitalized for mental illness three years ago. The hospital has now discharged her, and she is receiving follow-up treatment in an after-care clinic where she receives her medication. She wants her children back, and the clinic approves. The private agency, however, feels that the mother is not ready and also reports that the children do not want to go home.
Of the following, the BEST course of action for you, as a supervisor, to take is to

   A. recommend that the children be returned to their mother as soon as possible since the clinic approves
   B. keep the children in placement until the private agency feels that the mother is ready to cope with them and that they want to go back to her
   C. refer the case to your psychiatric consultant and be guided by his recommendation
   D. confer with representatives of the private agency and the clinic to determine if and when the children should be returned, and how to prepare the mother and children for eventual reunion

6. A child welfare worker in one of your units reports that a mother with whom she is working claims that the school is discriminating against her children because she is a welfare recipient. Her children have a history of truancy and poor school achievement. The child welfare worker feels that the mother's assessment of the situation has some validity.
Of the following, the BEST course of action for you to suggest to your worker is to

   A. support the mother's defense of her children and report the alleged discrimination on the part of the school to the Board of Education
   B. inquire further into the reasons for the children's truancy and poor achievement with the children, the mother, and school officials
   C. explore with the mother her feelings about receiving public assistance and encourage her to find a job so she won't need assistance
   D. disengage herself from her close involvement in this case since she has stopped being objective

7. It is standard practice, in providing service to children in their own homes, for the child welfare worker to work directly with the child when

   A. it is determined that his parents have no emotional problem
   B. his problems are primarily in the school and community
   C. he needs help in coping with his living situation and in accepting parental limitations
   D. his parents do not speak English and the worker needs an interpreter

8. Which one of the following statements regarding the provision of services to children in their own homes is CORRECT?

   A. The caretaking parent is the primary client.
   B. Services for the child under six are generally provided through the parents.
   C. The way the home is kept is of primary importance in evaluating the case.
   D. The most pertinent service is the one given directly to the child.

9. Of the following, the MOST important problem in the development of group day care services for infants is that this service

   A. requires many safeguards to protect the child's physical health and emotional development
   B. costs too much for the parents or the community to support
   C. cannot be licensed by the Board of Health or State Department of Social Services
   D. is looked upon by the community with disfavor because people, in general, feel that mothers should stay home with infants

10. A child welfare worker should offer day care services

    A. to every mother on her caseload
    B. to mothers on her caseload who have the necessary motivation and strength to work but must provide for the care of their children during the day
    C. only to those mothers on her caseload who are already working and could take their children out of placement if day care services were available
    D. only to parents who have several children and are receiving supplementary assis-

11. The one of the following which is an important, although not the primary, function of a homemaker, from the point of view of the child welfare agency, is to

    tance which could be cut off if the mother went to work
    A. interpret foster care services to the family
    B. provide the family with counseling services, as needed, in relation to the problems the homemaker encounters in her work with the family
    C. provide the child welfare worker with additional information about the family which might not be obtained otherwise, and which could be used in further planning with the family
    D. help the mother to understand her feelings of inadequacy as a parent and to face reality

12. A mother who is legally married to someone not the father of her illegitimate child wants to surrender the child legally for adoption. Her husband does not know about the child. The child welfare worker should advise her that she may have difficulty in legally surrendering the child unless she

    A. signs a surrender and swears her husband is not the child's father
    B. informs her husband about the child and can obtain his written denial of paternity
    C. tells the court the child's real father abandoned her and the child
    D. can prove that she and her husband cannot care for the child properly

13. In planning for the placement of a ten-year-old child in foster care, it is standard practice for the child welfare worker to

    A. make the decision with the parents, without including the child in the planning
    B. enlist the child's participation to the fullest extent possible, depending on his level of maturity
    C. have the parents take responsibility for preparing the child for placement
    D. help the child to accept the agency's and his parents' decision since he cannot do anything about it

14. Of the following, the MOST important reason that child welfare agencies should place more emphasis upon early case finding is in order to

    A. help more families obtain needed public assistance
    B. offer families more extensive diagnostic evaluation
    C. prevent separation of children from their parents
    D. provide more extensive referral services

15. If a parent accused of child neglect refuses protective service, the caseworker should inform him that

    A. he does not have the right to refuse protective service since this service is mandatory
    B. the child will be removed from the home as soon as a foster home can be found
    C. the problem may be referred to the jurisdiction of the Family Court as the result of his refusal
    D. any further complaints of child neglect against him will be investigated by the agency and reported to the police if substantiated

16. As a supervisor, you are asked to work on a committee which is planning for the appropriate use of case aides in family and child welfare programs.
    Of the following, the one which would be the LEAST appropriate assignment for a case aide is

    A. determining, as a result of interviewing the client, the best solution to his family problems
    B. helping a parent to attend an important school meeting by caring for his children at home during the meeting
    C. finding and suggesting recipes to make a client's medically required diet more appetizing and palatable
    D. visiting an overburdened parent's home in order to suggest how to divide some of the home chores among the children

17. As a Supervisor II, you observe that the two case aides assigned to your area, who attend school parttime, are not given many work assignments. You discuss this situation with the Supervisors I, who state that it is too time-consuming to design appropriate tasks for the case aides since they are not available for a full day's work. The Supervisors I express their willingness to have the case aides do their school assignments in the office.
    Of the following, your BEST response would be that the

    A. Supervisors I should see to it that the case aides do not do homework in the office because it would give the clients a bad impression
    B. Supervisors I must assign appropriate tasks to case aides so that the agency and its clients may derive the maximum benefit from their time on the job
    C. agency has great confidence in the use of parapro-fessionals
    D. schools are able to adjust their schedules for case aides and that Supervisors I should be able to do the same

18. As a supervisor, you are asked to help obtain assistance for a group of residents of your geographic area who have taken a number of unrelated children into their homes and are caring for them at their own expense.
Of the following, the MOST accurate information you can give this group is:

   A. There is no legal basis for meeting their requests
   B. Home Relief is not available as a means of providing for some of the cost of a child's care in a non-related home
   C. An ADC grant can be made for child care to friends of the child's parents who are now supporting the child
   D. They can apply to the Bureau of Child Welfare for certification as foster parents for these children and for payment of foster home boarding care rates

19. Mr. and Mrs. A are requesting the discharge from foster care of Mary, their eight-year-old daughter, who was placed voluntarily six weeks ago after the child told her teacher that Mr. A *bothered* her. Although Mary had given an elaborate account of this alleged sexual molestation, both parents denied that such an incident occurred, but requested placement as a way of relieving the tension in the home.
As the supervisor asked to participate in the decision about the parent's request for Mary's discharge from placement, your MAIN consideration should be

   A. the dynamics involved in differentiating between a child's fantasy and reality
   B. Mary's feelings about returning home to her family
   C. the factors that went into the earlier decision for placement
   D. that cases of alleged sexual molestation can be handled by court action only

20. As a supervisor on call for consultation on decisions to be made by the emergency night child welfare staff, you are asked to approve by telephone the discharge of a seven-year-old boy to his father. The boy had been admitted to a city children's shelter when his mother, who was separated from his father, died suddenly during surgery.
Of the following pieces of information supplied by the child welfare worker over the phone, which is the LEAST relevant to your decision? The

   A. father and child know each other
   B. child is in reasonably good health
   C. father has arranged with his mother to look after his son while he is at work
   D. father does not know whether the mother had initiated divorce proceedings

21. As a supervisor in the foster home program, you receive a request for a change of case worker from a foster mother who is caring for four adolescents. The mother complains that the case worker spends too much time with the children when he visits. In a conference with you, the Supervisor I, who had worked with this foster home until his recent promotion, states his belief that his positive relationship with the foster mother is more important than her relationship with the present case worker. He, therefore, wants to keep the foster home within his unit but assign it to a different case worker. He is concerned that any other course of action might result in the foster mother's request for removal of the children from her home.
Your conference with the Supervisor I on this situation should focus on the

   A. difficulty involved in securing homes for four adolescents
   B. rights of foster parents to request removal of foster children

C. rights of foster parents to request a different case worker
D. way in which the Supervisor I sees his enabling role

22. As the supervisor for the After Hours Emergency Child Care Services, you recognize, while reviewing the reports of the previous night's activities, the name of a five-year-old boy who had been reported as a runaway two weeks earlier. The current report again indicates that the police found the child wandering in the street at 3:00 A.M. about six blocks from his grandmother's house, where he has been living for the past six months. The current report also indicates that the grandmother arrived at the police station and took the boy home before any action was taken by the Emergency Child Care staff. Of the following, the LEAST valid focus for your next group conference with your staff in discussing this case would be to

   A. stress the advisability of placement of children referred for the second time in a two-week period
   B. discuss critical indices of potential difficulties that may be present when a five-year-old child is a chronic runaway
   C. review indices for referring emergency situations that are overtly resolved after hours to the regular unit the next day
   D. develop a workshop on how to interview children

23. As a Supervisor II in a Protective Services section, you are reviewing a case record forwarded to you by the Supervisor I of one of your units, to show you how promptly his case workers have been making field visits on new referrals. In this case, the case worker visited the home within an hour after receipt of an anonymous report of neglect of an infant. The record stated that the worker was impressed by the mother's politeness and the cleanliness of the home, that the allegation of neglect was false, and that no follow-up was indicated.
Of the following, your MAIN emphasis in reviewing this case material should be on

   A. determining how the case worker interpreted to the mother the reason for his visit
   B. finding out whether the baby was seen during the case worker's visit to the home
   C. planning to compliment the Supervisor I on having helped his caseworkers to make field visits promptly
   D. determining whether or not the record shows that the anonymous complaint was actually disproved

24. As a Supervisor II in an adoption program, you notice that the Supervisor I of one of your units presents about four times as many atypical situations for your review and approval as the Supervisor I of any other unit under your supervision.
Of the following, the BEST step for you take FIRST in order to evaluate the significance of this observation would be to

   A. recognize that, because many children are hard to place, no family that offers to adopt a child should be eliminated
   B. accept the fact that all atypical situations should be reviewed carefully because adoption policies are changing rapidly
   C. analyze the handling of all the studies initiated within this unit during a specific time span in order to determine if appropriate action has been taken in every case
   D. become aware that the supervisors of the other units are probably rejecting atypical situations without bringing them to your attention

25. As a supervisor, you read at night a newspaper report on a serious fire in an apartment building in your work area in which a number of children suffered from severe burns and smoke inhalation, and were admitted to X Hospital. The next morning, the MOST appropriate action for the district office to take would be to

    A. explore whether or not X Hospital sees evidence of abuse or neglect of any of the children hospitalized and, if so, whether the hospital plans to refer the children and families to the Bureau of Child Welfare
    B. initiate steps for referral for re-housing
    C. send a worker to the area to determine how or if he can be of help
    D. send a worker to the hospital to offer family and child welfare services

25.____

KEY (CORRECT ANSWERS)

1.	D	11.	C
2.	D	12.	B
3.	A	13.	B
4.	D	14.	C
5.	D	15.	C
6.	B	16.	A
7.	C	17.	B
8.	B	18.	D
9.	A	19.	C
10.	B	20.	D

21. D
22. A
23. D
24. C
25. A

TEST 3

DIRECTIONS: Each question or incomplete statement is followed by several suggested answers or completions. Select the one that BEST answers the question or completes the statement. *PRINT THE LETTER OF THE CORRECT ANSWER IN THE SPACE AT THE RIGHT.*

1. Of the following, the MOST important influence on the personality development of a child during the first year is the

   A. family as a whole
   B. mother
   C. way his siblings react to him
   D. relationship between the parents

2. Of the following, the terms which is GENERALLY applied to the situation in which an infant in foster care has insufficient interaction with a substitute mother is

   A. maternal rejection
   B. mothering complex
   C. maternal deprivation
   D. interaction deficiency

3. When a foster child exhibits nonconforming behavior, it is MOST important for the foster parents to be able to

   A. ignore this behavior since this is the child's way of expressing his emotional needs
   B. accept and condone this behavior as an expression of the child's insecurity
   C. use punishment and reward to force the child to conform
   D. accept this behavior without condoning it, while trying to meet the child's emotional needs

4. Separation of the infant from his mother can be a traumatic experience. The amount of emotional damage to the infant and the consequent effects on his personality depend MAINLY on the

   A. quality and consistency of the substitute mothering he receives
   B. reasons for and duration of the separation
   C. kind of preparation for separation the infant receives
   D. degree of the mother's acceptance of the placement

5. Research studies of language development in young children have shown that

   A. the multiple mothering of children in a large family retards language development
   B. language retardation in otherwise normal children is usually related to inadequate language stimulation
   C. language retardation is always associated with slow motor development
   D. children are usually slow in learning to talk when more than one language is spoken in the home

6. The two MOST important influences on the cultural development of a seven-year-old child are the

   A. home and peer group
   B. school and peer group
   C. home and school
   D. home and church

7. In our culture, a child gains his sense of identity MAINLY from
    A. knowledge about and experience with his parents and extended family
    B. association with members of his own ethnic group
    C. a study of the historical and ethnic factors in this culture
    D. association with his peers

8. A child who has grown up in foster care may want to talk about his natural parents, although he has never known them.
   Of the following, the BEST way for a child welfare worker to deal with this situation is to
    A. help the child to forget that he is a foster child and to relate to his foster parents as though they were his natural parents
    B. encourage the child to express his feelings and fantasies about his natural parents so that the worker can help his understand these feelings and fantasies
    C. set up a psychiatric interview for the child to determine if he is making a satisfactory adjustment to his foster child status
    D. tell the child that he can look for his natural parents when he is older

9. Of the following, the MOST important reason that those responsible for the care of a child in placement should never depreciate the child's natural parents or the home from which he came is that the
    A. child's self-esteem depends on how he feels about his natural parents and his previous experiences
    B. natural parents may have been incapable of being adequate parents
    C. child may feel that the substitute parents are jealous of his natural parents
    D. child will be forced into the position of defending his natural parents and will resent the substitute parents

10. The Children's Apperception Test (CAT) is a commonly used protective test for pre-school children in which the child
    A. has an opportunity to express his fantasies and moods through drawing and painting
    B. tells a story about pictures that are shown to him
    C. completes an unfinished story
    D. is given a variety of toys and is placed in a make-believe play situation

11. Sickle cell anemia is a blood disease MOST commonly found in children whose parents are
    A. Caucasian   B. interracial
    C. Black or Latin American D. Oriental

12. Schizophrenia in children USUALLY becomes manifest
    A. during the latency period
    B. during adolescence only
    C. when the mother has a history of schizophrenia
    D. during early childhood or adolescence

13. Although day care was originally established mainly as a social service for working mothers, it has been found that

    A. day care can also be an educational experience for a child and help in the development of peer relationships
    B. most working mothers would prefer to leave their children with friends or relatives rather than at a day care center
    C. it would be economically feasible to make day care centers available to all mothers in the community
    D. working mothers of physically and mentally handicapped children do not benefit from day care facilities

13._____

14. In deciding on which day care center to recommend to a working mother, the MOST important of the following considerations is the

    A. educational background of the staff
    B. ratio of staff to children
    C. director of the center
    D. physical plant and recreational facilities

14._____

15. During the past few years, dramatic and serious incidents of child abuse have resulted in

    A. the passage of legislation in all states requiring medical and other designated personnel to report incidents of abuse
    B. the proliferation of child care agencies dealing with child abuse cases only
    C. a tightening of restrictions in most states on eligibility for public assistance of parents who abuse their children
    D. a slight decline in the number of child neglect cases reported to authorities and a slight increase in the number of child abuse cases reported

15._____

16. Of the following alternatives, the one which is LEAST available to the Black unwed mother in planning for her child is

    A. adoption
    B. temporary care in a small group home
    C. foster family care
    D. dependence upon her family

16._____

Questions 17-19.

DIRECTIONS: Questions 17 through 19 are to be answered by matching each of the persons listed in Column I with the field in which the person is an authority, as stated in Column II.

COLUMN I

17. Lauretta Bender

18. Fritz Redl

19. Gisela Konopka

COLUMN II

A. Group work
B. Homefinding
C. Day care
D. Acting out, emotionally disturbed children and adolescents
E. Childhood schizophrenia

17._____

18._____

19._____

20. As a supervisor in the Division of Interagency Relationships, you become aware that a particular voluntary child-caring agency often reports discharges of children from foster care either on the date the discharge plan is to be implemented or shortly after the discharge has taken place. Your staff informs you that such late discharge reports are forwarded most frequently when the discharge plans indicate a need for intensive supportive help. The BEST approach for you to take would be to meet with

    A. your team and tell them to disapprove all such discharges in the future
    B. your team and tell them to take all appropriate clerical action as quickly as possible
    C. your immediate supervisor to inform him that a particular agency is making unsound discharges
    D. representatives of the voluntary child-caring agency to discuss the subject of discharge practice

21. As a supervisor, you are representing the Bureau of Child Welfare on a committee that meets bi-monthly to plan for the needs of retarded children. You note that the comments of the parents of retardates are warmly accepted at each session, but are never incorporated into the minutes or included in recommendations for follow-up action.
    Of the following, the BEST approach for you to take would be to

    A. report this discrepancy to your immediate supervisor
    B. attempt to maneuver the group so that the parents of retardates will be encouraged to make more comments at committee meetings
    C. raise a question at the next regular meeting about the discrepancy you have found in the recording of participation by parents
    D. talk to several parents after the next meeting to find out if they object to the manner in which minutes are recorded

22. As a Supervisor II, you note that your staff appears to make minimal use of community resources to meet client needs. When you discuss this at a staff meeting, you meet a great deal of resistance from both the Supervisors I and the case workers, who say: *You are not out there.*
    Of the following, your BEST response in this situation would be to

    A. refer to an article you have read about how workers can involve themselves in the community
    B. ask for volunteers for a committee to explore possible resources in the community they serve
    C. ask the group to give examples of their use of community resources
    D. ask the group to describe their experiences in seeking out community resources

23. As a supervisor, you are invited as an expert consultant to meet with a community group discussing child day care needs. At the meeting, one parent urges the establishment of group care for infants in her apartment building, where there are about ten infants between the ages of three and twelve months.
    Of the following, the FIRST suggestion you should make concerning this proposal is that

    A. those parents in the building who are interested in infant care attend a meeting to discuss the specific needs of his own infant and what his expectations of group care are

B. the group invite an expert on infant development to its next meeting for the purpose of outlining a possible infant group care program
C. the community group insure that pediatric consultation would be available to the persons providing the infant group care
D. one parent contact the landlord of the apartment building to inquire about regulations or stipulations for use of an apartment or other building facility for an infant group care program

24. Of the following, the MOST desirable pattern to utilize in community planning of child welfare services is to

    A. leave each agency in the community free to develop those services which its constituency feels strongly about and wishes to support
    B. have each agency in the community assigned a particular function by the state licensing authority in line with community need
    C. consult a central planning body, representative of all agencies in the community, when any agency is considering developing a new service or dropping an old one
    D. merge all agencies in the community providing like services, in order to reduce administrative expenses

25. It is recognized that very young children should not remain in hospitals after the condition for which they were admitted is under control and can be managed outside the hospital setting.
Of the following, the BEST method for preventing well children from remaining in hospitals longer than necessary is for

    A. hospital policy to provide for referral of children to the Bureau of Child Welfare when the hospital staff believe parents may not be able to take their children home as soon as they are medically well
    B. hospital social service departments to prepare social histories on children hospitalized, focusing especially on children *at risk*
    C. the public child welfare agency to receive on a regular basis lists of children remaining in hospitals
    D. hospitals to send to child caring agencies lists of children not discharged, although medically well

KEY (CORRECT ANSWERS)

1. B
2. C
3. D
4. A
5. B

6. C
7. A
8. B
9. A
10. B

11. C
12. D
13. A
14. B
15. A

16. A
17. E
18. D
19. A
20. D

21. C
22. D
23. A
24. C
25. A

EXAMINATION SECTION
TEST 1

DIRECTIONS: Each question or incomplete statement is followed by several suggested answers or completions. Select the one that BEST answers the question or completes the statement. *PRINT THE LETTER OF THE CORRECT ANSWER IN THE SPACE AT THE RIGHT.*

1. Assume that you are a supervisor. One of the workers under your supervision is careless about the routine aspects of his work.
   Of the following, the action MOST likely to develop in this worker a better attitude toward job routines is to demonstrate that

   A. it is just as easy to do his job the right way
   B. organization of his job will leave more time for field work
   C. the routine part of the job is essential to performing a good piece of work
   D. job routines are a responsibility of the worker

   1.____

2. A supervisor can MOST effectively secure necessary improvement in a worker's office work by

   A. encouraging the worker to keep abreast of his work
   B. relating the routine part of his job to the total job to be done
   C. helping the worker to establish a good system for covering his office work and holding him to it
   D. informing the worker that he will be required to organize his work more efficiently

   2.____

3. A supervisor should offer criticism in such a manner that the criticism is helpful and not overwhelming.
   Of the following, the LEAST valid inference that can be drawn on the basis of the above statement is that a supervisor should

   A. demonstrate that the criticism is partial and not total
   B. give criticism in such a way that it does not undermine the worker's self-confidence
   C. keep his relationships with the worker objective
   D. keep criticism directed towards general work performance

   3.____

4. The one of the following areas in which a worker may LEAST reasonably expect direct assistance from the supervisor is in

   A. building up rapport with all clients
   B. gaining insight into the unmet needs of clients
   C. developing an understanding of community resources
   D. interpreting agency policies and procedures

   4.____

5. You are informed that a worker under your supervision has submitted a letter complaining of an unfair service rating. Of the following, the MOST valid assumption for you to make concerning this worker is that he should be

   A. more adequately supervised in the future
   B. called in for a supervisory conference
   C. given a transfer to some other unit where he may be more happy
   D. given no more consideration than any other inefficient worker

   5.____

6. Assume that you are a supervisor. You find that a somewhat bewildered worker, newly appointed to the department, hesitates to ask questions for fear of showing his ignorance and jeopardizing his position.
Of the following, the BEST procedure for you to follow is to

   A. try to discover the reason for his evident fear of authority
   B. tell him that when he is in doubt about a procedure or a policy, he should consult his fellow workers
   C. develop with the worker a plan for more frequent supervisory conferences
   D. explain why each staff member is eager to give him any available information that will help him do a good job

7. Of the following, the MOST effective method of helping a newly appointed worker adjust to his new job is to

   A. assure him that with experience his uncertain attitudes will be replaced by a professional approach
   B. help him, by accepting him as he is, to have confidence in his ability to handle the job
   C. help him to be on guard against the development of punitive attitudes
   D. help him to recognize the mutability of the agency's policies and procedures

8. Suppose that, as a supervisor, you have scheduled an individual conference with an experienced worker under your supervision.
Of the following, the BEST plan of action for this conference is to

   A. discuss the cases that the worker is most interested in
   B. plan with the worker to cover the problems in his cases that are difficult for him
   C. advise the worker that the conference is his to do with as he sees fit
   D. spot check the worker's case load in advance and select those cases for discussion in which the worker has done poor work

9. Of the following, the CHIEF function of a supervisor should be to

   A. assist in the planning of new policies and the evaluation of existing ones
   B. promote congenial relationships among members of the staff
   C. achieve optimum functioning of each unit and each worker
   D. promote the smooth functioning of job routines

10. The competent supervisor must realize the importance of planning.
Of the following, the aspect of planning which is LEAST appropriately considered a responsibility of the supervisor is

    A. long-range planning for the proper functioning of his unit
    B. planning to take care of peak and slack periods
    C. planning to cover agency policies in group conferences
    D. long-range planning to develop community resources

11. The one of the following objectives which should be of LEAST concern to the supervisor in the performance of his duties is to

    A. help the worker to make friends with all of his clients
    B. be impartial and fair to all members of the staff
    C. stimulate the worker's growth on the job
    D. meet the needs of individual workers for case work guidance

12. The one of the following which is LEAST properly considered a direct responsibility of the supervisor is

    A. liaison between the staff and the administrator
    B. interpreting administrative orders and procedures to the worker
    C. training new workers
    D. maintaining staff morale at a high level

13. In order to teach the worker to develop an objective approach, the BEST action for the supervisor to take is to help the worker to

    A. develop a sincere interest in his job
    B. understand the varied responsibilities that are an integral part of his job
    C. differentiate clearly between himself as a friend and as a case worker
    D. find satisfaction in his work

14. If the worker shows excessive submission which indicates a need for dependence on the supervisor in handling a case, it would be MOST advisable for the supervisor to

    A. indicate firmly that the worker-supervisor relationship does not call for submission
    B. define areas of responsibility of worker and of supervisor
    C. recognize the worker's need to be sustained and supported and help him by making decisions for him
    D. encourage the worker to do his best to overcome his handicap

15. Assume that, as a supervisor, you are conducting a group conference.
    Of the following, the BEST procedure for you to follow in order to stimulate group discussion is to

    A. permit the active participation of all members
    B. direct the discussion to an acceptable conclusion
    C. resolve conflicts of opinion among members of the group
    D. present a question for discussion on which the group members have some knowledge or experience

16. Suppose that, as a new supervisor, you wish to inform the staff under your supervision of your methods of operation. Of the following, the BEST procedure for you to follow is to

    A. advise the staff that they will learn gradually from experience
    B. inform each worker in an individual conference
    C. call a group conference for this purpose
    D. distribute a written memorandum among all members of the staff

17. The MOST constructive and effective method of correcting a worker who has made a mistake is, in general, to

    A. explain that his evaluation is related to his errors
    B. point out immediately where he erred and tell him how it should have been done
    C. show him how to readjust his methods so as to avoid similar errors in the future
    D. try to discover by an indirect method why the error was made

18. The MOST effective method for the supervisor to follow in order to obtain the cooperation of a worker under his supervision is, wherever possible, to

    A. maintain a careful record of performance in order to keep the worker on his toes
    B. give the worker recognition in order to promote greater effort and give him more satisfaction in his work
    C. try to gain the worker's cooperation for the good of the welfare service
    D. advise the worker that his advancement on the job depends on his cooperation

19. Of the following, the MOST appropriate initial course for a worker to take when he is unable to clarify a policy with his supervisor is to

    A. bring up the problem at the next group conference
    B. discuss the policy immediately with his fellow workers
    C. accept the supervisor's interpretation as final
    D. determine what responsibility he has for putting the policy into effect

20. Good administration allows for different treatment of different workers.
    Of the following, the CHIEF implication of this statement is that

    A. it would be unfair for the supervisor not to treat all staff members alike
    B. fear of favoritism tends to undermine staff morale
    C. best results are obtained by individualization within the limits of fair treatment
    D. difficult problems call for a different kind of approach

21. The MOST effective and appropriate method of building efficiency and morale in a group of workers is, in general,

    A. by stressing the economic motive
    B. through use of the authority inherent in the position
    C. by a friendly approach to all
    D. by a discipline that is fair but strict

22. Of the following, the LEAST valid basis for the assignment of work to an employee is the

    A. kind of service to be rendered
    B. experience and training of the worker
    C. health and capacity of the worker
    D. racial composition of the community where the office is located

23. The CHIEF justification for staff education, consisting of in-service training, lies in its contribution to 23.____

    A. improvement in the quality of work performed
    B. recruitment of a better type of worker to the department
    C. employee morale, accruing from a feeling of growth on the job
    D. the satisfaction that the worker gets on his job

24. Suppose that you are a supervisor. A worker no longer with the department requests you, as his former supervisor, to write a letter recommending him for a position with a private organization. 24.____
    Of the following, the BEST procedure for you to follow is to include in the letter only information that

    A. will help the applicant get the job
    B. is clear, factual, and substantiated
    C. is known to you personally
    D. can readily be corroborated by personal interview

25. Of the following, the MOST important item on which to base the efficiency evaluation of a worker under your supervision is 25.____

    A. the nature of the relationship that he has built up with his clients
    B. how he gets along with his fellow employees
    C. his personal habits and skills
    D. the effectiveness of his control over his case load

KEY (CORRECT ANSWERS)

1.	D	11.	A
2.	B	12.	A
3.	D	13.	C
4.	A	14.	B
5.	B	15.	D
6.	C	16.	C
7.	B	17.	C
8.	B	18.	B
9.	C	19.	D
10.	D	20.	C

21. D
22. D
23. A
24. B
25. D

TEST 2

DIRECTIONS: Each question or incomplete statement is followed by several suggested answers or completions. Select the one that BEST answers the question or completes the statement. *PRINT THE LETTER OF THE CORRECT ANSWER IN THE SPACE AT THE RIGHT*

1. According to generally accepted personnel practice, the MOST effective method of building morale in a new worker is to   1._____

    A. exercise caution in praising the worker, lest he become overconfident
    B. give sincere and frank commendation whenever possible in order to stimulate interest and effort
    C. praise the worker highly even for mediocre performance so that he will be stimulated to do better
    D. warn the worker frequently that he cannot hope to succeed unless he puts forth his best effort

2. Errors made by newly appointed workers often follow a predictable pattern.   2._____
The one of the following errors likely to have LEAST serious consequences is the tendency of a new worker to

    A. discuss problems that are outside his province with the client
    B. persuade the client to accept the worker's solution of a problem
    C. be too strict in carrying out departmental policy and procedure
    D. depend upon the use of authority due to his inexperience and lack of skill in working with people

3. Of the following, the BEST method of helping the new worker to apply social case work principles is, in general, through   3._____

    A. the medium of the individual conference
    B. reading generally accepted authorities on the subject
    C. the medium of his own cases
    D. a course of study for him to follow

4. The MOST effective way for a supervisor to break down a worker's defensive stand against supervisory guidance is to   4._____

    A. come to an understanding with him on the mutual responsibilities involved in the job of the worker and supervisor
    B. tell him he must feel free to express his opinions and to discuss basic problems
    C. show him how to develop toward greater objectivity, sensitivity, and understanding
    D. advise him that it is necessary to carry out agency policy and procedures in order to do a good job

5. Of the following, the LEAST essential function of the supervisor who is conducting a group conference should be to   5._____

    A. keep attention focused on the purpose of the conference
    B. encourage discussion of controversial points
    C. make certain that all possible viewpoints are discussed
    D. be thoroughly prepared in advance

132

6. When conducting a group conference, the supervisor should be LEAST concerned with

    A. providing an opportunity for the free interchange of ideas
    B. imparting knowledge and understanding of case work
    C. leading the discussion toward a planned goal
    D. pointing out where individual workers have erred in case work practice

7. If the participants in a conference are unable to agree on the proper application of a concept to the work of the department, the MOST suitable temporary procedure for the supervisor to follow is to

    A. suggest that each member think the subject through before the next meeting
    B. tell the group to examine their differences for possible conflicts with present policies
    C. suggest that practices can be changed because of new conditions
    D. state the acceptable practice in the agency and whether deviations from such practice can be permitted

8. If a worker is to participate constructively in any group discussion, it is MOST important that he have

    A. advance notice of the agenda for the meeting
    B. long experience in the department
    C. knowledge and experience in social work
    D. the ability to assume a leadership role

9. Of the following, the MOST important principle for the supervisor to follow when conducting a group discussion is that he should

    A. move the discussion toward acceptance by the group of a particular point of view
    B. express his ideas clearly and succinctly
    C. lead the group to accept the authority inherent in his position
    D. contribute to the discussion from his knowledge and experience

10. The one of the following which is considered LEAST important as a purpose of the group conference is to

    A. provide for a free exchange of ideas among the members of the group
    B. evaluate case work methods and procedures in order to protect the members from individual criticism
    C. provide an opportunity to interpret procedures and general case work practices
    D. pool the experience of the group members for the benefit of all

11. In order for the evaluation conference to stimulate MOST effectively the worker's professional growth on the job, it should

    A. start him thinking about his present status with the agency
    B. show him the necessity for taking stock of his total performance
    C. give him a sense of direction in relation to his future development
    D. give him a better perspective on the work of the department

12. The PRIMARY consideration in good case recording is that the case history should

    A. be written simply and contain only significant and relevant material
    B. contain subjective material needed on the case
    C. be written concisely and clearly in good English
    D. include points of interest to both the worker and the supervisor

13. Of the following, the MOST important purpose of the case record summary in the department of welfare is to

    A. acquaint the worker with forgotten details of the case
    B. provide a review of the client's status and eligibility
    C. provide a detailed picture of what has happened in the case
    D. give the worker a new perspective on the case

14. The development of good public relations in the area for which the supervisor is responsible should be considered by the supervisor as

    A. not his responsibility as he is primarily responsible for his workers' services
    B. dependent upon him as he is in the best position to interpret the department to the community
    C. not important to the adequate functioning of the department
    D. a part of his method of carrying out his job responsibility as what his workers do affect the community

15. Assume that you are a supervisor. A newly appointed worker under your supervision asks you what action he should take when, finding it necessary to refuse relief to a client, the client becomes unusually belligerent and refuses to listen to reason.
    Of the following, the BEST advice for you to give the worker is to

    A. refer the client to the case supervisor
    B. explain to the client at length the reasons for the refusal
    C. carefully explore with the client all possible courses of action
    D. be firm and definite in his refusal

16. Of the following, the LEAST accurate statement concerning the relationship of public and private social agencies is that

    A. both have an important and necessary function to perform
    B. they are not to be considered as competing or rival agencies
    C. they are cooperating agencies
    D. their work is based on fundamentally different social work concepts

17. Of the following, the LEAST accurate statement concerning the worker-client relationship is that the worker should have the ability to

    A. express warmth of feeling in appropriate ways as a basis for a professional relationship which creates confidence
    B. feel appropriately in the relationship without losing the ability to see the situation in the perspective necessary to help the people immersed in it
    C. identify himself with the client so that the worker's personality does not influence the client
    D. use keen observation and perceive what is significant with a new range of appreciation of the meaning of the situation to the client

18. Of the following, the MOST fundamental psychological concept underlying case work in the public assistance field is that

    A. eligibility for public assistance should be reviewed from time to time
    B. workers should be aware of the prevalence of psychological disabilities among members of families on public assistance
    C. workers should realize the necessity of carrying out the policies laid down by the state office in order that state aid may be received
    D. in the process of receiving assistance, recipients should not be deprived of their normal status of self-direction

19. Of the following, the MOST comprehensive, as well as the MOST accurate, statement concerning the professional attitude of the social worker is that he should

    A. have a real concern for, and an intelligent interest in, the welfare of the client
    B. recognize that the client's feelings rather than the realities of his needs are of major importance to the client
    C. put at the client's service the worker's knowledge and sincere interest in him
    D. use his insight and understanding to make sound decisions about the client

20. The one of the following reasons for refusing a job which is LEAST acceptable, from the viewpoint of maintaining a client's continued rights to unemployment insurance benefits, is that

    A. acceptance of the job would interfere with the client's joining or retaining membership in a labor union
    B. there is a strike, lockout, or other industrial controversy in the establishment where employment is offered
    C. the distance from the place of employment to his home is greater than seems justified to the client
    D. the wages offered are lower than the prevailing wages in that locality

21. The one of the following statements concerning the division of veterans assistance which is LEAST accurate is that the service includes

    A. the arrangement of occupational registration, vocational rehabilitation, and employment referrals for veterans and their dependents
    B. aid in obtaining citizenship papers under special naturalization, laws applicable only to veterans
    C. the handling of claims for burial expenses of deceased honorably discharged veterans
    D. providing for hospital care and domiciliary care at soldiers' homes

22. Whenever possible, a client on home relief who is eligible for assistance under one of the three categories should be changed to categorical relief.
Of the following, the LEAST accurate statement regarding this change is that

    A. change to categorical relief increases public understanding of the purposes and functioning of relief
    B. change to categorical relief is in accordance with the plan of the state department of welfare
    C. the Federal government reimburses the state and city for a percentage under the categories
    D. the welfare client will be better served under one of the forms of categorical relief

23. The LEAST accurate of the following statements regarding the functions of the transportation unit of the department of welfare is that it

    A. provides transportation for persons who have verified offers of employment in states which border on New York State
    B. determines eligibility for payment of transportation expenses
    C. makes reservations and purchases tickets for blind clients who are leaving for temporary periods
    D. is authorized to furnish transportation to all those who meet requirements regardless of whether or not they are in receipt of public assistance

24. The PRIMARY purpose of the welfare department will be BEST fulfilled, insofar as the giving of public assistance is concerned, if the rules and regulations are interpreted

    A. to the end that the most economical operation of the department will result
    B. strictly according to written instructions
    C. with special consideration for those applicants having the greatest needs
    D. insofar as possible in line with each applicant's circumstances and needs

25. The National Mental Health Act provides for

    A. an appropriation of five million dollars for research on mental illness
    B. the organization of a National Mental Health Institution within the structure of the Public Health Service
    C. an appropriation of five million dollars for grants-in-aid to the states for research and expansion of training and clinical facilities
    D. the establishment of Mental Hygiene Clinics in certain specified areas

KEY (CORRECT ANSWERS)

1. B	6. D	11. C	16. D	21. D
2. C	7. D	12. A	17. C	22. D
3. C	8. A	13. B	18. D	23. A
4. A	9. D	14. D	19. C	24. D
5. B	10. B	15. D	20. C	25. B

EXAMINATION SECTION
TEST 1

DIRECTIONS: Each question or incomplete statement is followed by several suggested answers or completions. Select the one that BEST answers the question or completes the statement. *PRINT THE LETTER OF THE CORRECT ANSWER IN THE SPACE AT THE RIGHT.*

1. One of the responsibilities of the supervisor is to provide top administration with information about clients and their problems that will help in the evaluation of existing policies and indicate the need for modifications. In order to fulfill this responsibility, it would be MOST essential for the supervisor to

    A. routinely forward all regularly prepared and recurrent reports from his subordinates to his immediate superior
    B. regularly review agency rules, regulations, and policies to make sure that he has sufficient knowledge to make appropriate analyses
    C. note repeated instances of failure of staff to correctly administer a policy and schedule staff conferences for corrective training
    D. analyze reports on cases submitted by subordinates in order to select relevant trend material to be forwarded to his superiors

2. You find that your division has a serious problem because of unusually long delays in filing reports and overdue approvals to private agencies under contract for services. The MOST appropriate step to take FIRST in this situation would be to

    A. request additional staff to work on reports and approvals
    B. order staff to work overtime until the backlog is eliminated
    C. impress staff with the importance of expeditious handling of reports and approvals
    D. analyze present procedures for handling reports and approvals

3. When a supervisor finds that he must communicate orally information that is significant enough to affect the entire staff, it would be MOST important to

    A. distribute a written summary of the information to his staff before discussing it orally
    B. tell his subordinate supervisors to discuss this information at individual conferences with their subordinates
    C. call a follow-up meeting of absentees as soon as they return
    D. restate and summarize the information in order to make sure that everyone understands its meaning and implications

4. Of the following, the BEST way for a supervisor to assist a subordinate who has unusually heavy work pressures is to

    A. point out that such pressures go with the job and must be tolerated
    B. suggest to him that the pressures probably result from poor handling of his workload
    C. help him to be selective in deciding on priorities during the period of pressure
    D. ask him to work overtime until the period of pressure is over

5. Leadership is a basic responsibility of the supervisor. The one of the following which would be the LEAST appropriate way to fulfill this role is for the supervisor to

   A. help staff to work up to their capacities in every possible way
   B. encourage independent judgment and actions by staff members
   C. allow staff to participate in decisions within policy limits
   D. take over certain tasks in which he is more competent than his subordinates

6. Assume that you have assigned a very difficult administrative task to one of your best subordinate supervisors, but he is reluctant to take it on because he fears that he will fail in it. It is your judgment, however, that he is quite capable of performing this task.
   The one of the following which is the MOST desirous way for you to handle this situation is to

   A. reassure him that he has enough skill to perform the task and that he will not be penalized if he fails
   B. reassign the task to another supervisor who is more achievement-oriented and more confident of his skills
   C. minimize the importance of the task so that he will feel it is safe for him to attempt it
   D. stress the importance of the task and the dependence of the other staff members on his succeeding in it

7. Assume that a member of your professional staff deliberately misinterprets a new state directive because he fears that its enforcement will have an adverse effect on clients. Although you consider him to be a good supervisor and basically agree with him, you should direct him to comply. Of the following, the MOST desirable way for you to handle this situation would be to

   A. avoid a confrontation with him by transferring responsibility for carrying out the directive to another member of your staff
   B. explain to him that you are in a better position than he to assess the implications of the new directive
   C. discuss with him the basic reasons for his misinterpretation and explain why he must comply with the directive
   D. allow him to interpret the directive in his own way as long as he assumes full responsibility for his actions

8. Of the following, the MAIN reason it is important for an administrator in a large organization to properly coordinate the work delegated to subordinates is that such coordination

   A. makes it unnecessary to hold frequent staff meetings and conferences with key staff members
   B. reduces the necessity for regular evaluation of procedures and programs, production, and performance of personnel
   C. results in greater economy and stricter accountability for the organization's resources
   D. facilitates integration of the contributions of the numerous staff members who are responsible for specific parts of the total workload

9. The one of the following which would NOT be an appropriate reason for the formulation of an entirely new policy is that it would

A. serve as a positive affirmation of the agency's function and how it is to be carried out
B. give focus and direction to the work of the staff, particularly in decision-making
C. inform the public of the precise conditions under which services will be rendered
D. provide procedures which constitute uniform methods of carrying out operations

10. Of the following, it is MOST difficult to formulate policy in an organization where

    A. work assignments are narrowly specialized by units
    B. staff members have varied backgrounds and a wide range of competency
    C. units implementing the same policy are in the same geographic location
    D. staff is experienced and fully trained

11. For a supervisor to feel that he is responsible for influencing the attitudes of his staff members is GENERALLY considered

    A. *undesirable;* attitudes of adults are emotional factors which usually cannot be changed
    B. *desirable;* certain attitudes can be obstructive and should be modified in order to provide effective service to clients
    C. *undesirable;* the supervisor should be nonjudgmental and accepting of widely different attitudes and social patterns of staff members
    D. *desirable;* influencing attitudes is a teaching responsibility which the supervisor shares with the training specialist

12. The one of the following which is NOT generally a function of the higher-level supervisor is

    A. projecting the budget and obtaining financial resources
    B. providing conditions conducive to optimum employee production
    C. maintaining records and reports as a basis for accountability and evaluation
    D. evaluating program achievements and personnel effectiveness in accordance with goals and standards

13. As a supervisor in a recently decentralized services center offering multiple services, you are given responsibility for an orientation program for professional staff on the recent reorganization of the department.
    Of the following, the MOST appropriate step to take FIRST would be to

    A. organize a series of workshops for subordinate supervisors
    B. arrange a tour of the new geographic area of service
    C. review supervisors' reports, statistical data, and other relevant material
    D. develop a resource manual for staff on the reorganized center

14. Experts generally agree that the content of training sessions should be closely related to workers' practice. Of the following, the BEST method of achieving this aim is for the training conference leader to

    A. encourage group discussion of problems that concern staff in their practice
    B. develop closer working relationships with top administration
    C. coordinate with central office to obtain feedback on problems that concern staff
    D. observe workers in order to develop a pattern of problems for class discussion

15. The one of the following which is generally the MOST useful teaching tool for professional staff development is

    A. visual aids and tape recordings
    B. professional literature
    C. agency case material
    D. lectures by experts

16. The one of the following which is NOT a good reason for using group conferences as a method of supervision is to

    A. give workers a feeling of mutual support through sharing common problems
    B. save time by eliminating the need for individual conferences
    C. encourage discussion of certain problems that are not as likely to come up in individual conferences
    D. provide an opportunity for developing positive identification with the department and its programs

17. The supervisor, in his role as teacher, applies his teaching in line with his understanding of people and realizes that teaching is a highly individualized process, based on understanding of the worker as a person and as a learner.
    This statement implies MOST NEARLY that the supervisor must help the worker to

    A. overcome his biases
    B. develop his own ways of working
    C. gain confidence in his ability
    D. develop the will to work

18. Of the following, the circumstances under which it would be MOST appropriate to divide a training conference for professional staff into small workshops is when

    A. some of the trainees are not aware of the effect of their attitudes and behavior on others
    B. the trainees need to look at human relations problems from different perspectives
    C. the trainees are faced with several substantially different types of problems in their job assignments
    D. the trainees need to know how to function in many different capacities

19. Of the following, the MAIN reason why it is important to systematically evaluate a specific training program while it is in progress is to

    A. collect data that will serve as a valid basis for improving the agency's overall training program and maintaining control over its components
    B. insure that instruction by training specialists is conducted in a manner consistent with the planned design of the training program
    C. identify areas in which additional or remedial training for the training specialists can be planned and implemented
    D. provide data which are usable in effecting revisions of specific components of the training program

20. Staff development has been defined as an educational process which seeks to provide agency staff with knowledge about specific job responsibilities and to effect changes in staff attitudes and behavior patterns. Assume that you are assigned to define the educational objectives of a specific training program.
    In accordance with the above concept, the MOST helpful formulation would be a statement of the

    A. purpose and goals of each training session
    B. generalized patterns of behavior to be developed in the trainees
    C. content material to be presented in the training sessions
    D. kind of behavior to be developed in the trainees and the situations in which this behavior will be applied

21. In teaching personnel under your supervision how to gather and analyze facts before attempting to solve a problem, the one of the following training methods which would be MOST effective is

    A. case study
    B. role playing
    C. programmed learning
    D. planned experience

22. Federal and state welfare agencies have been discussing the importance of analyzing functions traditionally included in the position of caseworker, with a view toward identifying and separating those activities to be performed by the most highly skilled personnel.
    Of the following, an IMPORTANT secondary gain which can result from such differential use of staff is that

    A. supporting job assignments can be given to persons unable to meet the demands of casework, to the satisfaction of all concerned
    B. documentation will be provided on workers who are not suited for all the duties now part of the caseworker's job
    C. caseworkers with a high level of competence in working with people can be rewarded through promotion or merit increases
    D. incompetent workers can be identified and categorized as a basis for transfer or separation from the service

23. Of the following, a serious DISADVANTAGE of a performance evaluation system based on standardized evaluation factors is that such a system tends to

    A. exacerbate the anxieties of those supervisors who are apprehensive about determining what happens to another person
    B. subject the supervisor to psychological stress by emphasizing the incompatibility of his dual role as both judge and counselor
    C. create organizational conflict by encouraging personnel who wish to enhance their standing to become too aggressive in the performance of their duties
    D. lead many staff members to concentrate on measuring up in terms of the evaluation factors and to disregard other aspects of their work

24. Which of the following would contribute MOST to the achievement of conformity of staff activities and goals to the intent of agency policies and procedures?

    A. Effective communications and organizational discipline
    B. Changing nature of the underlying principles and desired purpose of the policies and procedures

C. Formulation of specific criteria for implementing the policies and procedures
D. Continuous monitoring of the essential effectiveness of agency operations

25. Job enlargement, a management device used by large organizations to counteract the adverse effects of specialization on employee performance, is LEAST likely to improve employee motivation if it is accomplished by

A. lengthening the job cycle and adding a large number of similar tasks
B. allowing the employee to use a greater variety of skills
C. increasing the scope and complexity of the employee's job
D. giving the employee more opportunities to make decisions

KEY (CORRECT ANSWERS)

1.	D	11.	B
2.	D	12.	A
3.	D	13.	A
4.	C	14.	A
5.	D	15.	C
6.	A	16.	B
7.	C	17.	B
8.	D	18.	C
9.	D	19.	A
10.	B	20.	D

21. A
22. A
23. D
24. A
25. A

TEST 2

DIRECTIONS: Each question or incomplete statement is followed by several suggested answers or completions. Select the one that BEST answers the question or completes the statement. *PRINT THE LETTER OF THE CORRECT ANSWER IN THE SPACE AT THE RIGHT.*

1. When a supervisor requires approval for case action on a higher level, the process used is known as

    A. administrative clearance
    B. going outside channels
    C. administrative consultation
    D. delegation of authority

    1.____

2. In delegating authority to his subordinates, the one of the following to which a good supervisor should give PRIMARY consideration is the

    A. results expected of them
    B. amount of power to be delegated
    C. amount of responsibility to be delegated
    D. their skill in the performance of present tasks

    2.____

3. Of the following, the type of decision which could be SAFELY delegated to lower-level staff without undermining basic supervisory responsibility is one which

    A. involves a commitment that can be fulfilled only over a long period of time
    B. has fairly uncertain goals and promises
    C. has the possibility of modification built into it
    D. may generate considerable resistance from those affected by it

    3.____

4. Of the following, the MOST valuable contribution made by the informal organization in a large public service agency is that such an organization

    A. has goals and values which are usually consistent with and reinforce those of the formal organization
    B. is more flexible than the formal organization and more adaptable to changing conditions
    C. has a communications system which often contributes to the efficiency of the formal organization
    D. represents a sound basis on which to build the formal organizational structure

    4.____

5. Of the following, the condition under which it would be MOST useful for a social services agency to develop detailed procedures is when

    A. subordinate supervisory personnel need a structure to help them develop greater independence
    B. employees have little experience or knowledge of how to perform certain assigned tasks
    C. coordination of agency activities is largely dependent upon personal contact
    D. agency activities must continually adjust to changes in local circumstances

    5.____

6. Assume that a certain public agency administrator has the management philosophy that his agency's responsibility is to routinize existing operations, meet each day's problems as they arise, and resolve problems with a minimun of residual effect upon himself or his agency.
The possibility that this official would be able to administer his agency without running into serious difficulties would be MORE likely during a period of

   A. economic change
   B. social change
   C. economic crisis
   D. social and economic stability

7. Some large organizations have adopted the practice of allowing each employee to establish his own performance goals, and then later evaluate himself in an individual conference with his immediate supervisor.
Of the following, a DRAWBACK of this approach is that the employee

   A. may set his goals too low and rate himself too highly
   B. cannot control those variables which may improve his performance
   C. has no guidelines for improving his performance
   D. usually finds it more difficult to criticize himself than to accept criticism from others

8. Decentralization of services cannot completely eliminate the requirement of central office approval for certain case actions.
The MOST valid reason for complaint about this requirement is that

   A. unavoidable delay created by referral to central office may cause serious problems for the client
   B. it may lower morals of supervisors who are not given the authority to take final action on urgent cases
   C. the concept of role responsibility is minimized
   D. the objective of delegated responsibility tends to be negated

9. Which of the following would be the MOST useful administrative tool for the purpose of showing the sequence of operations and staff involved?
A(n)

   A. organization chart
   B. flow chart
   C. manual of operating procedures
   D. statistical review

10. The prevailing pattern of organization in large public agencies consists of a limited span of control and organization by function or, at lower levels, process.
Of the following, the PRINCIPAL effect which this pattern or organization has on the management of work is that it

   A. reduces the management burden in significant ways
   B. creates a time lag between the perception of a problem and action on it
   C. makes it difficult to direct and observe employee performance
   D. facilitates the development of employees with managerial ability

11. The one of the following which would be the MOST appropriate way to reduce tensions between line and staff personnel in public service agencies is to

    A. provide in-service training that will increase the sensitivity of line and staff personnel to their respective roles
    B. assign to staff personnel the role of providing assistance only when requested by line personnel
    C. separate staff from line personnel and provide staff with its own independent reward structure
    D. give line and staff personnel equal status in making decisions

12. In determining the appropriate span of control for subordinate supervisors, which of the following principles should be followed?
    The more

    A. complex the work, the broader the effective span of control
    B. similar the jobs being supervised, the more narrow the effective span of control
    C. interdependent the jobs being supervised, the more narrow the effective span of control
    D. unpredictable the work, the broader the effective span of control

13. A method sometimes used in public service agencies to improve upward communication is to require subordinate supervisory staff to submit to top management monthly narrative reports of any problems which they deem important for consideration.
    Of the following, a MAJOR disadvantage of this method is that it may

    A. enable subordinate supervisors to avoid thinking about their problems by simply referring such matters to their superiors
    B. obscure important issues so that they are not given appropriate attention
    C. create a need for numerous staff conferences in order to handle all of the reported problems
    D. encourage some subordinate supervisors to focus on irrelevant matters and compete with each other in the length and content of their reports

14. The use of a committee as an approach to the problem of coordinating interdepartmental activities can present difficulties if the committee functions PRIMARILY as a(n)

    A. means of achieving personal objectives and goals
    B. instrument for coordinating activities that flow across departmental lines
    C. device for involving subordinate personnel in the decision-making process
    D. means of giving representation to competing interest groups

15. A study was recently made of the attitudes and perceptions of a sample of public assistance workers in nine New Jersey county welfare boards who had experienced a major organizational change and redefinition of their jobs as a result of separation of the income maintenance and social services functions. Questionnaires administered to these workers indicated that a disproportionate number of workers in the larger agencies were dissatisfied with the reorganization and their new assignments. Of the following, the MOST plausible reason for this dissatisfaction is that workers in larger agencies are

A. less likely to be known to management and to be personally disciplined if they expressed dissatisfaction with their new roles
B. less likely to have the opportunity to participate in planning a reorganization and to be given consideration for the assignments they preferred
C. given a shorter lead period to implement the change and, therefore, had insufficient time to plan the reorganization and carry it out efficiently
D. usually made up of more older members who have had routinized their work according to habit and find it more difficult to adjust to change

16. An article which recently appeared in a professional journal presents a proposal for participatory leadership in which the goal of supervision would be development of subordinates' self-reliance, with the premise that each staff member is held accountable for his own performance. The one of the following which would NOT be a desirable outcome of this type of supervision is the

    A. necessity for subordinates to critically examine their performance
    B. development by some subordinates of skills not possessed by the supervisor
    C. establishment of a quality control unit for sample checking and identification of errors
    D. relaxation of demands made on the supervisor

17. The *management by objectives* concept is a major development in the administration of human services organizations. The purpose of this approach is to establish a system for

    A. reduction of waiting time
    B. planning and controlling work output
    C. consolidation of organizational units
    D. work measurement

18. Assume that you encounter a serious administrative problem in implementing a new program. After consulting with members of your staff individually, you come up with several alternate solutions.
    Of the following, the procedure which would be MOST appropriate for evaluating the relative merits of each solution would be to

    A. try all of them on a limited experimental basis
    B. break the problem down into its component parts and analyze the effect of each solution on each component in terms of costs and benefits
    C. break the problem down into its component parts, eliminate all intangibles, and measure the effect of the tangible aspects of each solution on each component in terms of costs and benefits
    D. bring the matter before your weekly staff conference, discuss the relative merits of each alternate solution, and then choose the one favored by the majority of the conference

19. When establishing planning objectives for a service program under your supervision, the one of the following principles which should be followed is that objectives

    A. are rarely verifiable if they are qualitative
    B. should be few in number and of equal importance
    C. should cover as many of the activities of the program as possible
    D. should be set in the light of assumptions about future funding

20. Assume that you have been assigned responsibility for coordinating various aspects of the case aide program in a community social services center.
Which of the following administrative concepts would NOT be applicable to this assignment?

    A. Functional job analysis
    B. Peer group supervision
    C. Differential use of staff
    D. Systems design

21. Good administrative practice includes the use of outside consultants as effective technique in achieving agency objectives.
However, the one of the following which would NOT be an appropriate role for the consultant is

    A. provision of technical or professional expertise not otherwise available in the agency
    B. administrative direction of a new program activity
    C. facilitating coordination and communication among agency staff
    D. objective measurement of the effectiveness of agency services

22. Of the following, the MOST common fault of recent research projects attempting to measure the effectiveness of social programs has been their

    A. questionable methodology
    B. inaccurate findings
    C. unrealistic expectations
    D. lack of objectivity

23. One of the most difficult tasks of supervision in a modern public agency is teaching workers to cope with the hostile reactions of clients.
In order to help the disconcerted worker analyze and understand a client's hostile behavior, the supervisor should FIRST

    A. encourage the worker to identify with the client's frustrations and deprivations
    B. give the worker a chance to express and accept his feelings about the client
    C. ask the worker to review his knowledge of the client and his circumstances
    D. explain to the worker that the client's anger is not directed at the worker personally

24. Determination of the level of participation, or how much of the public should participate in a given project, is a vital step in community organization.
In order to make this determination, the FIRST action that should be taken is to

    A. develop the participants
    B. fix the goals of the project
    C. evaluate community interest in the project
    D. enlist the cooperation of community leaders

25. The one of the following which would be the MOST critical factor for successful operation of a decentralized system of social programs and services is

    A. periodic review and evaluation of services delivered at the community level
    B. transfer of decision-making authority to the community level wherever feasible
    C. participation of indigenous non-professionals in service delivery
    D. formulation of quantitative plans for dealing with community problems wherever feasible

KEY (CORRECT ANSWERS)

1. A
2. A
3. C
4. C
5. B

6. D
7. A
8. A
9. B
10. B

11. A
12. C
13. D
14. A
15. B

16. D
17. B
18. C
19. D
20. B

21. B
22. C
23. B
24. B
25. B

EXAMINATION SECTION
TEST 1

DIRECTIONS: Each question or incomplete statement is followed by several suggested answers or completions. Select the one that BEST answers the question or completes the statement. *PRINT THE LETTER OF THE CORRECT ANSWER IN THE SPACE AT THE RIGHT.*

1. It is generally accepted that, of the following, the MOST important medium for developing integration and continuity in learning on the job is
   A. day-to-day experience on the job
   B. the supervisory conference
   C. the staff meeting
   D. the professional seminar

   1.____

2. Assume that you find that one of your workers is over-identifying with a particular client.
   Of the following, the MOST appropriate step for you to take FIRST in dealing with this situation is to
   A. transfer the cases to another worker
   B. inform the worker that he cannot give satisfactory service if he over-identifies with a client
   C. interview the client yourself to determine his feelings about his relationship with the worker
   D. arrange a conference with the worker to discuss the reasons for her over-identification with this client

   2.____

3. The one of the following which is the MOST likely reason why a newly-appointed supervisor would have a tendency to interfere actively in a relationship between one of his workers and a client is that the supervisor
   A. has unresolved feelings about relinquishing the role of worker, and has not yet accepted his role as supervisor
   B. must give direct assistance in the situation because the worker cannot handle it
   C. is attempting to share with his worker the knowledge and skill which he has developed in direct practice
   D. has not realized that immediate responsibility for work with clients has been delegated to others

   3.____

4. A worker who has a tendency to resist authority and supervision can be helped MOST effectively if, of the following, the supervisor
   A. behaves in a strict and impersonal manner so that the worker will accept his authority as a supervisor
   B. modifies the relationship so that he will be less authoritarian and threatening to the worker
   C. gives the worker a simple, matter-of-fact interpretation of the supervisory relationship and has an understanding acceptance of the worker's response
   D. temporarily establishes a peer relationship with the worker in order to overcome his resistance

   4.____

5. Before interviewing a newly-appointed worker for the first time, of the following, it is DESIRABLE for the supervisor to
   A. learn as much as he can about the worker's background and interests in order to eliminate the routine of asking questions and eliciting answers
   B. review the job information to be covered in order to make it easier to be impersonal and keep to the business at hand
   C. send the worker orientation material about the agency and the job and ask him to study it before the interview
   D. review available information about the worker in order to find an area of shared experience to serve as a *taking off* point for getting acquainted

6. In interviewing a new worker, of the following, it is IMPORTANT for the supervisor to
   A. give direction to the progress of the interview and maintain a leadership role throughout
   B. allow the worker to take the initiative in order to give him full scope for freedom of expression
   C. maintain a non-directional approach so that the worker will reveal his true attitudes and feelings
   D. avoid interrupting the worker, even though he seems to want to do all the talking

7. When a new worker, during his first few days, shows such symptoms of insecurity as *stage fright*, helpless immobility, or extreme talkativeness, of the following, it would be MOST helpful for the supervisor to
   A. start the worker out on some activity in which he is relatively secure
   B. ignore the symptoms and allow the worker to *sink or swim* on his own
   C. have a conference with the worker and interpret to him the reasons for his feelings of insecurity
   D. consider the probability that this worker may not be suited for a profession which requires skill in interpersonal relationships

8. Of the following, the MOST desirable method of minimizing workers' dependence on the supervisor and encouraging self-dependence is to
   A. hold group instead of individual supervisory conferences at regular intervals
   B. schedule individual supervisory conferences only in response to the workers' obvious need for guidance
   C. plan for progressive exposure to other opportunities for learning afforded by the agency and the community
   D. allow workers to learn by trial and error rather than by direct supervisory guidance

9. Of the following, it would NOT be appropriate for the supervisor to use early supervisory conferences with the new workers as a means of
   A. giving him direct practical help in order to get going on the job
   B. estimating the level of his native abilities, professional skills and experience
   C. getting clues as to his characteristic ways of learning in a new situation
   D. assessing his potential for future supervisory responsibility

10. Without careful planning by the supervisor for orientation of the new worker, an informal system of orientation by co-workers inevitably develops.
Such an informal system of orientation is USUALLY
    A. *beneficial*, because many new workers learn more readily when instructed by their peers
    B. *harmful*, because informal orientation by an undesignated co-worker can lead a new worker astray instead of helping him
    C. *beneficial*, because assumption by subordinates of responsibility for orientation will free the supervisor for other urgent work
    D. *harmful*, because such informal orientation by a co-worker will tend to destroy the authority of the supervisor

10.____

11. Of the following, the BEST way for a supervisor to assist a subordinate who has unusual work pressures is to
    A. relieve him of some of his cases until the pressures subside
    B. help him to decide which cases should be given the most attention during the period of pressure, and how to provide coverage for less urgent cases
    C. inform him that he must learn to tolerate and adjust to such pressures
    D. point out that he should learn to understand the causes of the pressures, which probably resulted from his own deficiencies

11.____

12. Many supervisors have a tendency to use case records mainly for the purpose of analysis of the workers' skill or evaluation of their performance.
Of the following, a PROBABLE result of this practice is that
    A. workers are likely to tie-in recording with supervisory evaluation of their work, without giving proper emphasis to their importance in improving service to clients
    B. the worker is likely to devote an inordinate amount of time to case records at the expense of his clients
    C. the records are likely to be too lengthy and detailed, limiting their value for other important purposes
    D. the records are likely to be of little value for administrative and research purposes

12.____

13. A common obstacle to adequate recording in a large social work agency is the fact that many workers consider recording to be a time-consuming chore.
In order to obtain the cooperation of staff in keeping proper records, of the following, it is MOST important for an agency to provide
    A. indisputable evidence of the intelligent use of records as tools in formulating policy and improving service
    B. a system of checks and controls to assure that workers are preparing adequate and timely records
    C. adequate clerical services and mechanical equipment for recording
    D. sufficient time for recording in the organization of every job

13.____

14. The one of the following which is NOT a purpose of keeping case records in an agency is
    A. planning   B. research
    C. training   D. job classification

14.____

15. When a supervisor is reviewing the records of a worker, of the following, he should plan to read
    A. records of new cases only, following up each interview selectively
    B. the total caseload, in order to determine which aspects of the worker's performance should be examined
    C. those records which the worker has brought to the supervisor's attention because of the need for help
    D. a block of records selected according to the worker's need for help, and some records selected at random

16. The one of the following which is the PRIMARY purpose of the regular staff meeting in an agency is
    A. initiation of action in order to get the agency's work done
    B. staff training and development
    C. program and policy determination
    D. communication of new policies and procedures

17. Of the following, group supervision in an agency is intended as a means of
    A. strengthening the total supervisory process
    B. shifting the focus of supervision from the individual to the group
    C. saving costs in terms of time and manpower
    D. influencing policy through group interaction

18. The supervisor's job brings him closer to such limiting factors in the operation of an agency as faulty administrative structure, shortage of funds and lack of facilities, inadequacies in personnel practices, community pressures, and excessive workload.
    For the supervisor to make a practice of communicating to his subordinates his feelings of frustration about such limitations in the work setting would be
    A. *appropriate*, because the worker will be more understanding of the supervisor's burdens and frustrations
    B. *inappropriate*, because the climate created will block rather than further the purposes of supervision
    C. *appropriate*, because such communication will create a more democratic climate between the worker and the supervisor
    D. *inappropriate*, because the supervisor must support and condone agency policies and practices in the presence of subordinates

19. A suggestion has been made that the teaching and administrative functions of supervision should be separated, so that the supervisor responsible for teaching would not be responsible for evaluation of the same workers.
    The one of the following which is the MOST important reason for this point of view is that
    A. elements that confer on the supervisor a position of authority and power unduly threaten the learning situation
    B. teaching skill and administrative ability do not usually go together

C. a supervisor who has been responsible for training a worker is likely to be prejudiced in his favor
D. performance evaluation and total job accountability should be two separate functions

20. In reviewing a worker's cases in preparation for a periodic evaluation, you note that she has done a uniformly good job with certain types of cases and poor work with other types of cases.
Of the following, the BEST approach for you to take in this situation is to
    A. bring this to the worker's attention, find out why she favors certain types of clients, and discuss ways in which she can improve her service to all clients
    B. bring this to the worker's attention and suggest that she may need professional counseling, as she seems to be blocked in working with certain types of cases
    C. assign to her mainly those cases which she handles best and transfer the types of cases which she handles poorly to another worker
    D. accept the fact that a worker cannot be expected to give uniformly good service to all clients, and take no further action

20.____

KEY (CORRECT ANSWERS)

1.	B		11.	B
2.	D		12.	A
3.	A		13.	A
4.	C		14.	D
5.	D		15.	D
6.	A		16.	A
7.	A		17.	A
8.	C		18.	B
9.	D		19.	A
10.	B		20.	A

TEST 2

DIRECTIONS: Each question or incomplete statement is followed by several suggested answers or completions. Select the one that BEST answers the question or completes the statement. *PRINT THE LETTER OF THE CORRECT ANSWER IN THE SPACE AT THE RIGHT.*

1. Of the following, the choice of method to be used in the supervisory process should be influenced MOST by the
    A. number and type of cases carried by each worker
    B. emotional maturity of the worker
    C. number of workers supervised and their past experience
    D. subject matter to be learned and the long-range goals of supervision

1.____

2. In an evaluation conference with a worker, the BEST approach for the supervisor to take is to
    A. help the worker to identify his strengths as a basis for working on his weaknesses
    B. identify the worker's weaknesses and help him overcome them
    C. allow the worker to identify his weaknesses first and then suggest ways of overcoming them
    D. discuss the worker's weaknesses but emphasize his strengths

2.____

3. Assume that a worker is discouraged about the progress of his work and feels that it is futile to attempt to cope with many of his cases.
   Of the following, it would be BEST for the supervisor to
    A. suggest to the worker that such feelings are inappropriate for a professional worker
    B. tell the worker that he must seek professional help in order to overcome these feelings
    C. reduce the worker's caseload and give him cases that are less complex
    D. review with the worker several of his cases in which there were obvious accomplishments

3.____

4. The supervisor is responsible for providing the worker with the following means of support, with the EXCEPTION of
    A. interest and advice on his personal problems
    B. instruction on community resources
    C. inspiration for carrying out the work of the agency
    D. understanding his strengths and limitations

4.____

5. When a worker frequently takes the initiative in asking questions and discussing problems during a supervisory conference, this is PROBABLY an indication that the
    A. supervisor is not sufficiently interested in the work
    B. conference is a positive learning experience for the worker
    C. worker is hostile and resists supervision
    D. supervisor's position of authority is in question

5.____

6. When a supervisor finds that one of his workers cannot accept criticism, of the following, it would be BEST for the supervisor to
    A. have the worker transferred to another supervisor
    B. warn the worker of disciplinary proceedings unless his attitude changes
    C. have the worker suspended after explaining the reason
    D. explore with the worker his attitude toward authority

7. Of the following, the condition which the inexperienced worker is LEAST likely to be aware of, without the guidance of the supervisor, is
    A. when he is successful in helping a client
    B. when he is not making progress in helping a client
    C. that he has a personal bias toward certain clients
    D. that he feels insecure because of lack of experience

8. The supervisor should provide an inexperienced worker with controls as well as freedom MAINLY because controls will
    A. enable him to set up his own controls sooner
    B. put him in a situation which is closer to the realities of life
    C. help him to use authority in handling a casework problem
    D. give him a feeling of security and lay the foundation for future self-direction

9. A result of the use of summarized case recording by the worker is that it
    A. gives the supervisor more responsibility for selecting cases to discuss in conference
    B. makes more time available for other activities
    C. lowers the morale of many workers
    D. decreases discussion of cases by the worker and the supervisor

10. The distinction between the role of professional workers and the role of auxiliary or sub-professional workers in an agency is based upon the
    A. position within the agency hierarchy
    B. amount of close supervision given
    C. emergent nature of tasks assigned
    D. functions performed

11. Of the following, the MOST important source of learning for the worker should be
    A. departmental directives and professional literature
    B. his co-workers in the agency
    C. the content of in-service training courses
    D. the clients in his caseload

12. A client is MOST likely to feel that he is receiving acceptance and understanding if the social worker
    A. gets detailed information about the client's problem
    B. demonstrates that he realistically understands the client's problem
    C. has an intellectual understanding of the client's problem
    D. offers the client assurance of assistance

13. A client will be MORE encouraged to speak freely about his problems if the worker
    A. avoids asking too many questions
    B. asks leading rather than pointed questions
    C. suggests possible answers
    D. identifies with the client

14. A client would be MOST likely to be able to accept help in a time of crisis and need if the worker
    A. explains agency policy to him
    B. responds immediately to the client's need
    C. explains why help cannot be given immediately
    D. reaches out to help the client establish his rightful claim for assistance

15. It is a generally accepted principle that the worker should interpret for himself what the client is saying, but usually should not pass his interpretation on to the client because the client
    A. will become hostile to the worker
    B. should arrive at his own conclusions at his own pace
    C. must request the interpretation first
    D. usually wants facts, rather than the worker's interpretation

16. In evaluating the client's capacity to cope with his problems, it is MOST important for the worker to assess his ability to
    A. form close relationships
    B. ask for help
    C. express his hostility
    D. verbalize his difficulties

17. When a worker finds that he disagrees strongly with an agency policy, it is DESIRABLE for him to
    A. share his feelings about the policy with his client
    B. understand fully why he has such strong feelings about the policy
    C. refer cases involving the policy to his supervisor
    D. refuse to give help in cases involving the policy

18. Which of the following practices is BEST for a supervisor to use when assigning work to his staff?
    A. Give workers with seniority the most difficult jobs
    B. Assign all unimportant work to the slower workers
    C. Permit each employee to pick the job he prefers
    D. Make assignments based on the workers' abilities

19. In which of the following instances is a supervisor MOST justified in giving commands to people under his supervision?
    When
    A. they delay in following instructions which have been given to them clearly
    B. they become relaxed and slow about work, and he wants to speed up their production
    C. he must direct them in an emergency situation
    D. he is instructing them on jobs that are unfamiliar to them

20. Which of the following supervisory actions or attitudes is MOST likely to result in getting subordinates to try to do as much work as possible for a supervisor?
He
    A. shows that his most important interest is in schedules and production goals
    B. consistently pressures his staff to get the work out
    C. never fails to let them know he is in charge
    D. considers their abilities and needs while requiring that production goals be met

20.____

KEY (CORRECT ANSWERS)

1.	D	11.	D
2.	A	12.	B
3.	D	13.	D
4.	A	14.	D
5.	B	15.	B
6.	D	16.	A
7.	C	17.	B
8.	D	18.	D
9.	B	19.	C
10.	D	20.	D

TEST 3

DIRECTIONS: Each question or incomplete statement is followed by several suggested answers or completions. Select the one that BEST answers the question or completes the statement. *PRINT THE LETTER OF THE CORRECT ANSWER IN THE SPACE AT THE RIGHT.*

1. One of your workers comes to you and complains in an angry manner about your having chosen him for some particular assignment. In your opinion, the subject of the complaint is trivial land unimportant, but it seems to be quite important to your worker.
   The BEST of the following actions for you to take in this situation is to
   A. allow the worker to continue talking until he has calmed down and then explain the reasons for your having chosen him for that particular assignment
   B. warn the worker to moderate his tone of voice at once because he is bordering on insubordination
   C. tell the worker in a friendly tone that he is making a tremendous fuss over an extremely minor matter
   D. point out to the worker that you are his immediate supervisor and that you are running the unit in accordance with official policy

1.____

2. The one of the following which is the LEAST desirable action for an assistant supervisor to take in disciplining a subordinate for an infraction of the rules is to
   A. caution him against repetition of the infraction, even if it is minor
   B. point out his progress in applying the rules at the same time that you reprimand him
   C. be as specific as possible in reprimanding him for rule infractions
   D. allow a cooling-off period to elapse before reprimanding him

2.____

3. A training program for workers assigned to the intake section should include actual practice in simulated interviews under simulated conditions.
   The one of the following educational principles which is the CHIEF justification for this statement is that
   A. the workers will remember what they see better and longer than what they read or hear
   B. the workers will learn more effectively by actually doing the act themselves than they would learn from watching others do it
   C. the conduct of simulated interviews once or twice will enable them to cope with the real situation with little difficulty
   D. a training program must employ methods of a practical nature if the workers are to find anything of lasting value in it

3.____

4. In order for a supervisor to employ the system of democratic leadership in his supervision, it would generally be BEST for him to
   A. allow his subordinates to assist in deciding on methods of work performance and job assignments but only in those areas where decisions have not been made on higher administrative levels

4.____

B. allow his subordinates to decide how to do the required work, interposing his authority when work is not completed on schedule or is improperly completed
C. attempt to make assignments of work to individuals only of the type which they enjoy doing
D. maintain control over job assignment and work production, but allow the subordinates to select methods of work and internal conditions of work at democratically conducted staff conferences

5. In a unit in which supervision has been considered quite effective, it has become necessary to press for above-normal production for a limited period to achieve a required goal.
The one of the following which is a LEAST likely result of this pressure is that
    A. there will be more *griping* by employees
    B. some workers will do both more and better work than has been normal for them
    C. there will be an enhanced feeling of group unity
    D. there will be increased absenteeism

6. For a supervisor to encourage competitive feelings among his staff is
    A. *advisable*, chiefly because the workers will perform more efficiently when they have proper motivation
    B. *inadvisable*, chiefly because the workers will not perform well under the pressure of competition
    C. *advisable*, chiefly because the workers will have a greater incentive to perform their job properly
    D. *inadvisable*, chiefly because the workers may focus their attention on areas where they excel and neglect other essential aspects of the job

7. In selecting jobs to be assigned to a new worker, the supervisor should assign those jobs which
    A. give the worker the greatest variety of experience
    B. offer the worker the greatest opportunity to achieve concrete results
    C. present the worker with the greatest stimulation because of their interesting nature
    D. require the least amount of contact with outside agencies

8. A supervisor should avoid a detailed discussion of a worker-client interview with a new worker before the worker has fully recorded the interview CHIEFLY because such a discussion might
    A. cover matters which are already fully covered and explained in the written record
    B. make the worker forget some important deal learned during the interview
    C. color the recording according to the worker's reaction to his supervisor's opinions
    D. minimize the worker's feeling of having reached a decision independently

5._____

6._____

7._____

8._____

9. Some supervisors encourage their worker to submit a list of their questions about specific jobs or their comments about problems they wish to discuss in advance of the worker-supervisor conference.
This practice is
   A. *desirable*, chiefly because it helps to stimulate and focus the worker's thinking about his caseload
   B. *undesirable*, chiefly because it will stifle the worker's free expression of his problems and attitudes
   C. *desirable,* chiefly because it will allow the conference to move along more smoothly and quickly
   D. *undesirable*, chiefly because it will restrict the scope of the conference and the variety of jobs discussed

10. An alert supervisor hears a worker apparently giving the wrong information to a client and immediately reprimands him severely.
For the supervisor to reprimand the worker at his point is poor CHIEFLY because
   A. instruction must precede correct performance
   B. oral reprimands are less effective than written reprimands
   C. the worker was given no opportunity to explain his reasons for what he did
   D. more effective training can be obtained by discussing the errors with a group of workers

11. The one of the following circumstances when it would generally be MOST proper for a supervisor to do a job himself rather than to train a subordinate to do the job is when it is
   A. a job which the supervisor enjoys doing and does well
   B. not a very time-consuming job but an important one
   C. difficult to train another to do the job, yet is not difficult for the supervisor to do
   D. unlikely that this or any similar job will have to be done again at any future time

12. Effective training of subordinates requires that the supervisor understand certain facts about learning and forgetting processes.
Among these is the fact that people GENERALLY
   A. forget what they learned at a much greater rate during the first day than during subsequent periods
   B. both learn and forget at a relatively constant rate and this rate is dependent upon their general intellectual capacity
   C. learn at a relatively constant rate except for periods of assimilation when the quantity of retained learning decreases while information is becoming firmly fixed in the mind
   D. learn very slowly at first when introduced to a new topic, after which there is a great increase in the rate of learning

13. It has been suggested that a subordinate who likes his superior will tend to do better work than one who does not.
    According to the MOST widely held current theories of supervision, this suggestion is a
    A. *bad* one, since personal relationships tend to interfere with proper professional relationships
    B. *bad* one, since the strongest motivating factors are fear and uncertainty
    C. *good* one, since liking one's superior is a motivating factor for good work performance
    D. *good* one, since liking one's supervisor is the most important factor in employee performance

14. One factor which might be given consideration in deciding upon the optimum span of control of a supervisor over his immediate subordinates is the position of the supervisor in the hierarchy of the organization.
    It is generally considered proper that the number of subordinates immediately supervised by a higher, upper echelon supervisor _____ the number supervised by lower level supervisors.
    A. is unrelated to and tends to form no pattern with
    B. should be about the same as
    C. should be larger than
    D. should be smaller than

15. The one of the following instances when it is MOST important for an upper level supervisor to follow the chain of command is when he is
    A. communicating decisions
    B. communicating information
    C. receiving suggestions
    D. seeking information

16. At the end of his probationary period, a supervisor should be considered potentially valuable in his position if he shows
    A. awareness of his areas of strength and weakness, identification with the administration of the department, and ability to learn under supervision
    B. skill in work, supervision, and administration, and a friendly democratic approach to the staff
    C. knowledge of departmental policies and procedures and ability to carry them out, ability to use authority, and ability to direct the work of the staff
    D. an identification with the department, acceptance of responsibility, and ability to give help to the individuals who are to be supervised

17. Good supervision is selective because
    A. it is not necessary to direct all the activities of the person
    B. a supervisor would never have time to know the whole caseload of a worker
    C. workers resent too much help from a supervisor
    D. too much reading is a waste of valuable time

18. An important administrative problem is how precisely to define the limits of authority that is delegated to subordinate supervisors.
Such definition of limits of authority should be
    A. as precise as possible and practicable in all areas
    B. as precise as possible and practicable in areas of function, but should allow considerable flexibility in the area of personnel management
    C. as precise as possible and practicable in the area
    D. of personnel management, but should allow considerable flexibility in the areas of function
    E. in general terms so as to allow considerable flexibility both in the areas of function and in the areas of personnel management

18.____

19. Experts in the field of personnel relations feel that it is generally a bad practice for subordinate employees to become aware of pending or contemplated changes in policy or organizational set-up via the *grapevine* CHIEFLY because
    A. evidence that one or more responsible officials have proved untrustworthy will undermine confidence in the agency
    B. the information disseminated by this method is seldom entirely accurate and generally spreads needless unrest among the subordinate staff
    C. the subordinate staff may conclude that the administration feels the staff cannot be trusted with the true information
    D. the subordinate staff may conclude that the administration lacks the courage to make an unpopular announcement through official channels

19.____

20. Supervision is subject to many interpretations, depending on the area in which it functions.
Of the following, the statement which represents the MOST appropriate meaning of supervision as it is known in social work practice is that it
    A. is a leadership process for the development of new leaders
    B. is an educational and administrative process aimed at teaching personnel the goal of improved service to the client
    C. is an activity aimed chiefly at insuring that workers will adhere to all agency directives
    D. provides the opportunity for administration to secure staff reaction to agency policies

20.____

21. A supervisor may utilize various methods in the supervisory process.
The one of the following upon which sound supervisory practice rests in the selection of supervisory techniques is
    A. an estimate of the worker arrived at through current and past evaluation of performance as well as through worker's participation
    B. the previous supervisor's evaluation and recommendation
    C. the worker's expression of his personal preference for certain types of experience
    D. the amount of time available to supervisor and supervisee

21.____

22. It is the practice of some supervisors, when they believe that it would be desirable for a subordinate to take a particular action in a case, to inform the subordinate of this in the form of a suggestion rather than in the form of a direct order.
In general, this method of getting a subordinate to take the desired action is
    A. *inadvisable*; it may create in the mind of the subordinate the impression that the supervisor is uncertain about the efficacy of her plan and is trying to avoid whatever responsibility she may have in resolving the case
    B. *advisable*; it provides the subordinate with the maximum opportunity to use her own judgment in handling the case
    C. *inadvisable*; it provides the subordinate with no clear-cut direction and, therefore, is likely to leave her with a feeling of uncertainty and frustration
    D. *advisable*; it presents the supervisor's view in a manner which will be most likely to evoke the subordinate's cooperation

23. A veteran supervisor noticed that one of her workers of average ability had begun developing some bad work habits, becoming especially careless in her recordkeeping. After reprimand from the supervisor, the investigator corrected her errors and has been doing satisfactory work since then.
For the supervisor to keep referring to this period of poor work during her weekly conferences with this employee would generally be considered poor personnel practice CHIEFLY because
    A. praise rather than criticism is generally the best method to use in improving the work of an unsatisfactory worker
    B. the supervisor cannot know whether the employee's errors will follow an established pattern
    C. the fault which evoked the original negative criticism no longer exists
    D. this would tend to frustrate the worker by making her strive overly hard to reach a level of productivity which is beyond her ability to achieve

24. Assume that you are now a supervisor in a specific unit. Two experienced investigators in your unit, both of whom do above average work, have for some time not gotten along with each other for personal reasons Their attitude toward one another has suddenly become hostile and noisy disagreement has taken place in the office.
The BEST action for you to take FIRST in this situation is to
    A. transfer one of the two investigators to another unit where contact with the other investigator will be unnecessary
    B. discuss the problem with the two investigators together, insisting that they confide in you and tell you the cause of their mutual antagonism
    C. confer with the two investigators separately, pointing out to each the need to adopt an adult professional attitude with respect to their on-the-job relations
    D. advise the two investigators that should the situation grow worse, disciplinary action will be considered

25. It has long been recognized that relationships exist between worker morale and working conditions.
The one of the following which BEST clarifies these existing relationships is that morale is
   A. affected for better or worse in direct relationship to the magnitude of the changes in working conditions for better or worse
   B. better when working conditions are better
   C. little affected by working conditions so long as the working conditions do not approach the intolerable
   D. more affected by the degree of interest shown in providing good working conditions than by the actual conditions and may, perversely, be highest when working conditions are worst

25.____

KEY (CORRECT ANSWERS)

1.	A		11.	D
2.	D		12.	A
3.	B		13.	C
4.	A		14.	D
5.	D		15.	A
6.	D		16.	D
7.	B		17.	A
8.	C		18.	A
9.	A		19.	B
10.	C		20.	B

21. A
22. D
23. C
24. C
25. D

PHILOSOPHY, PRINCIPLES, PRACTICES, AND TECHNICS
OF
SUPERVISION, ADMINISTRATION, MANAGEMENT, AND ORGANIZATION

TABLE OF CONTENTS

	Page
MEANING OF SUPERVISION	1
THE OLD AND THE NEW SUPERVISION	1
THE EIGHT (8) BASIC PRINCIPLES OF THE NEW SUPERVISION	1
I. Principle of Responsibility	1
II. Principle of Authority	2
III. Principle of Self-Growth	2
IV. Principle of Individual Worth	2
V. Principle of Creative Leadership	2
VI. Principle of Success and Failure	2
VII. Principle of Science	3
VIII. Principle of Cooperation	3
WHAT IS ADMINISTRATION?	3
I. Practices Commonly Classed as "Supervisory"	3
II. Practices Commonly Classed as "Administrative"	3
III. Practices Commonly Classed as Both "Supervisory" and "Administrative"	4
RESPONSIBILITIES OF THE SUPERVISOR	4
COMPETENCIES OF THE SUPERVISOR	4
THE PROFESSIONAL SUPERVISOR-EMPLOYEE RELATIONSHIP	4
MINI-TEXT IN SUPERVISION, ADMINISTRATION, MANAGEMENT, AND ORGANIZATION	5
I. Brief Highlights	5
A. Levels of Management	6
B. What the Supervisor Must Learn	6
C. A Definition of Supervision	6
D. Elements of the Team Concept	6
E. Principles of Organization	6
F. The Four Important Parts of Every Job	7
G. Principles of Delegation	7
H. Principles of Effective Communications	7
I. Principles of Work Improvement	7
J. Areas of Job Improvement	7
K. Seven Key Points in Making Improvements	8

	L.	Corrective Techniques for Job Improvement	8
	M.	A Planning Checklist	8
	N.	Five Characteristics of Good Directions	9
	O.	Types of Directions	9
	P.	Controls	9
	Q.	Orienting the New Employee	9
	R.	Checklist for Orienting New Employees	9
	S.	Principles of Learning	10
	T.	Causes of Poor Performance	10
	U.	Four Major Steps in On-the-Job Instructions	10
	V.	Employees Want Five Things	10
	W.	Some Don'ts in Regard to Praise	11
	X.	How to Gain Your Workers' Confidence	11
	Y.	Sources of Employee Problems	11
	Z.	The Supervisor's Key to Discipline	11
	AA.	Five Important Processes of Management	12
	BB.	When the Supervisor Fails to Plan	12
	CC.	Fourteen General Principles of Management	12
	DD.	Change	12
II.	Brief Topical Summaries		13
	A.	Who/What is the Supervisor?	13
	B.	The Sociology of Work	13
	C.	Principles and Practices of Supervision	14
	D.	Dynamic Leadership	14
	E.	Processes for Solving Problems	15
	F.	Training for Results	15
	G.	Health, Safety, and Accident Prevention	16
	H.	Equal Employment Opportunity	16
	I.	Improving Communications	16
	J.	Self-Development	17
	K.	Teaching and Training	17
		1. The Teaching Process	17
		a. Preparation	17
		b. Presentation	18
		c. Summary	18
		d. Application	18
		e. Evaluation	18
		2. Teaching Methods	18
		a. Lecture	18
		b. Discussion	18
		c. Demonstration	19
		d. Performance	19
		e. Which Method to Use	19

PHILOSOPHY, PRINCIPLES, PRACTICES, AND TECHNICS
OF
SUPERVISION, ADMINISTRATION, MANAGEMENT, AND ORGANIZATION

MEANING OF SUPERVISION

The extension of the democratic philosophy has been accompanied by an extension in the scope of supervision. Modern leaders and supervisors no longer think of supervision in the narrow sense of being confined chiefly to visiting employees, supplying materials, or rating the staff. They regard supervision as being intimately related to all the concerned agencies of society, they speak of the supervisor's function in terms of "growth," rather than the "improvement" of employees.

This modern concept of supervision may be defined as follows: Supervision is leadership and the development of leadership within groups which are cooperatively engaged in inspection, research, training, guidance, and evaluation.

THE OLD AND THE NEW SUPERVISION

TRADITIONAL
1. Inspection
2. Focused on the employee
3. Visitation
4. Random and haphazard
5. Imposed and authoritarian
6. One person usually

MODERN
1. Study and analysis
2. Focused on aims, materials, methods, supervisors, employees, environment
3. Demonstrations, intervisitation, workshops, directed reading, bulletins, etc.
4. Definitely organized and planned (scientific)
5. Cooperative and democratic
6. Many persons involved (creative)

THE EIGHT (8) BASIC PRINCIPLES OF THE NEW SUPERVISION

I. Principle of Responsibility
   Authority to act and responsibility for acting must be joined.
   A. If you give responsibility, give authority.
   B. Define employee duties clearly.
   C. Protect employees from criticism by others.
   D. Recognize the rights as well as obligations of employees.
   E. Achieve the aims of a democratic society insofar as it is possible within the area of your work.
   F. Establish a situation favorable to training and learning.
   G. Accept ultimate responsibility for everything done in your section, unit, office, division, department.
   H. Good administration and good supervision are inseparable.

II. Principle of Authority
The success of the supervisor is measured by the extent to which the power of authority is not used.
   A. Exercise simplicity and informality in supervision
   B. Use the simplest machinery of supervision
   C. If it is good for the organization as a whole, it is probably justified.
   D. Seldom be arbitrary or authoritative.
   E. Do not base your work on the power of position or of personality.
   F. Permit and encourage the free expression of opinions.

III. Principle of Self-Growth
The success of the supervisor is measured by the extent to which, and the speed with which, he is no longer needed.
   A. Base criticism on principles, not on specifics.
   B. Point out higher activities to employees.
   C. Train for self-thinking by employees to meet new situations.
   D. Stimulate initiative, self-reliance, and individual responsibility
   E. Concentrate on stimulating the growth of employees rather than on removing defects.

IV. Principle of Individual Worth
Respect for the individual is a paramount consideration in supervision.
   A. Be human and sympathetic in dealing with employees.
   B. Don't nag about things to be done.
   C. Recognize the individual differences among employees and seek opportunities to permit best expression of each personality.

V. Principle of Creative Leadership
The best supervision is that which is not apparent to the employee.
   A. Stimulate, don't drive employees to creative action.
   B. Emphasize doing good things.
   C. Encourage employees to do what they do best.
   D. Do not be too greatly concerned with details of subject or method.
   E. Do not be concerned exclusively with immediate problems and activities.
   F. Reveal higher activities and make them both desired and maximally possible.
   G. Determine procedures in the light of each situation but see that these are derived from a sound basic philosophy.
   H. Aid, inspire, and lead so as to liberate the creative spirit latent in all good employees.

VI. Principle of Success and Failure
There are no unsuccessful employees, only unsuccessful supervisors who have failed to give proper leadership.
   A. Adapt suggestions to the capacities, attitudes, and prejudices of employees.
   B. Be gradual, be progressive, be persistent.
   C. Help the employee find the general principle; have the employee apply his own problem to the general principle.
   D. Give adequate appreciation for good work and honest effort.
   E. Anticipate employee difficulties and help to prevent them.
   F. Encourage employees to do the desirable things they will do anyway.
   G. Judge your supervision by the results it secures.

VII. Principle of Science
Successful supervision is scientific, objective, and experimental. It is based on facts, not on prejudices.
 A. Be cumulative in results.
 B. Never divorce your suggestions from the goals of training.
 C. Don't be impatient of results.
 D. Keep all matters on a professional, not a personal, level.
 E. Do not be concerned exclusively with immediate problems and activities.
 F. Use objective means of determining achievement and rating where possible.

VIII. Principle of Cooperation
Supervision is a cooperative enterprise between supervisor and employee.
 A. Begin with conditions as they are.
 B. Ask opinions of all involved when formulating policies.
 C. Organization is as good as its weakest link.
 D. Let employees help to determine policies and department programs.
 E. Be approachable and accessible—physically and mentally.
 F. Develop pleasant social relationships.

WHAT IS ADMINISTRATION

Administration is concerned with providing the environment, the material facilities, and the operational procedures that will promote the maximum growth and development of supervisors and employees. (Organization is an aspect and a concomitant of administration.)

There is no sharp line of demarcation between supervision and administration; these functions are intimately interrelated and, often, overlapping. They are complementary activities.

I. Practices Commonly Classed as "Supervisory"
 A. Conducting employees' conferences
 B. Visiting sections, units, offices, divisions, departments
 C. Arranging for demonstrations
 D. Examining plans
 E. Suggesting professional reading
 F. Interpreting bulletins
 G. Recommending in-service training courses
 H. Encouraging experimentation
 I. Appraising employee morale
 J. Providing for intervisitation

II. Practices Commonly Classified as "Administrative"
 A. Management of the office
 B. Arrangement of schedules for extra duties
 C. Assignment of rooms or areas
 D. Distribution of supplies
 E. Keeping records and reports
 F. Care of audio-visual materials
 G. Keeping inventory records
 H. Checking record cards and books

    I.   Programming special activities
    J.   Checking on the attendance and punctuality of employees

III.   Practices Commonly Classified as Both "Supervisory" and "Administrative"
    A.   Program construction
    B.   Testing or evaluating outcomes
    C.   Personnel accounting
    D.   Ordering instructional materials

RESPONSIBILITIES OF THE SUPERVISOR

A person employed in a supervisory capacity must constantly be able to improve his own efficiency and ability. He represent the employer to the employees and only continuous self-examination can make him a capable supervisor.

Leadership and training are the supervisor's responsibility. An efficient working unit is one in which the employees work with the supervisor. It is his job to bring out the best in his employees. He must always be relaxed, courteous, and calm in his association with his employees. Their feelings are important, and a harsh attitude does not develop the most efficient employees.

COMPETENCES OF THE SUPERVISOR

    I.   Complete knowledge of the duties and responsibilities of his position.
    II.   To be able to organize a job, plan ahead, and carry through.
    III.   To have self-confidence and initiative.
    IV.   To be able to handle the unexpected situation and make quick decisions.
    V.   To be able to properly train subordinates in the positions they are best suited for.
    VI.   To be able to keep good human relations among his subordinates.
    VII.   To be able to keep good human relations between his subordinates and himself and to earn their respect and trust.

THE PROFESSIONAL SUPERVISOR-EMPLOYEE RELATIONSHIP

There are two kinds of efficiency: one kind is only apparent and is produced in organizations through the exercise of mere discipline; this is but a simulation of the second, or true, efficiency which springs from spontaneous cooperation. If you are a manager, no matter how great or small your responsibility, it is your job, in the final analysis, to create and develop this involuntary cooperation among the people whom you supervise. For, no matter how powerful a combination of money, machines, and materials a company may have, this is a dead and sterile thing without a team of willing, thinking, and articulate people to guide it.

The following 21 points are presented as indicative of the exemplary basic relationship that should exist between supervisor and employee:

1. Each person wants to be liked and respected by his fellow employee and wants to be treated with consideration and respect by his superior.
2. The most competent employee will make an error. However, in a unit where good relations exist between the supervisor and his employees, tenseness and fear do not exist. Thus, errors are not hidden or covered up, and the efficiency of a unit is not impaired.

3. Subordinates resent rules, regulations, or orders that are unreasonable or unexplained.
4. Subordinates are quick to resent unfairness, harshness, injustices, and favoritism.
5. An employee will accept responsibility if he knows that he will be complimented for a job well done, and not too harshly chastised for failure; that his supervisor will check the cause of the failure, and, if it was the supervisor's fault, he will assume the blame therefore. If it was the employee's fault, his supervisor will explain the correct method or means of handling the responsibility.
6. An employee wants to receive credit for a suggestion he has made, that is used. If a suggestion cannot be used, the employee is entitled to an explanation. The supervisor should not say "no" and close the subject.
7. Fear and worry slow up a worker's ability. Poor working environment can impair his physical and mental health. A good supervisor avoids forceful methods, threats, and arguments to get a job done.
8. A forceful supervisor is able to train his employees individually and as a team, and is able to motivate them in the proper channels.
9. A mature supervisor is able to properly evaluate his subordinates and to keep them happy and satisfied.
10. A sensitive supervisor will never patronize his subordinates.
11. A worthy supervisor will respect his employees' confidences.
12. Definite and clear-cut responsibilities should be assigned to each executive.
13. Responsibility should always be coupled with corresponding authority.
14. No change should be made in the scope or responsibilities of a position without a definite understanding to that effect on the part of all persons concerned.
15. No executive or employee, occupying a single position in the organization, should be subject to definite orders from more than one source.
16. Orders should never be given to subordinates over the head of a responsible executive. Rather than do this, the officer in question should be supplanted.
17. Criticisms of subordinates should, whoever possible, be made privately, and in no case should a subordinate be criticized in the presence of executives or employees of equal or lower rank.
18. No dispute or difference between executives or employees as to authority or responsibilities should be considered too trivial for prompt and careful adjudication.
19. Promotions, wage changes, and disciplinary action should always be approved by the executive immediately superior to the one directly responsible.
20. No executive or employee should ever be required, or expected, to be at the same time an assistant to, and critic of, another.
21. Any executive whose work is subject to regular inspection should, wherever practicable, be given the assistance and facilities necessary to enable him to maintain an independent check of the quality of his work.

MINI-TEXT IN SUPERVISION, ADMINISTRATION, MANAGEMENT, AND ORGANIZATION

I. Brief Highlights

Listed concisely and sequentially are major headings and important data in the field for quick recall and review.

A. Levels of Management
Any organization of some size has several levels of management. In terms of a ladder, the levels are:

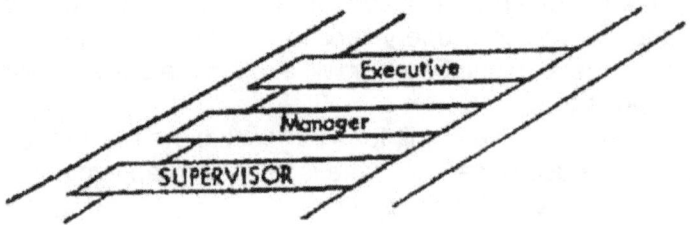

The first level is very important because it is the beginning point of management leadership.

B. What the Supervisor Must Learn
A supervisor must learn to:
1. Deal with people and their differences
2. Get the job done through people
3. Recognize the problems when they exist
4. Overcome obstacles to good performance
5. Evaluate the performance of people
6. Check his own performance in terms of accomplishment

C. A Definition of Supervisor
The term supervisor means any individual having authority, in the interests of the employer, to hire, transfer, suspend, lay-off, recall, promote, discharge, assign, reward, or discipline other employees or responsibility to direct them, or to adjust their grievances, or effectively to recommend such action, if, in connection with the foregoing, exercise of such authority is not of a merely routine or clerical nature but requires the use of independent judgment.

D. Elements of the Team Concept
What is involved in teamwork? The component parts are:
1. Members
2. A leader
3. Goals
4. Plans
5. Cooperation
6. Spirit

E. Principles of Organization
1. A team member must know what his job is.
2. Be sure that the nature and scope of a job are understood.
3. Authority and responsibility should be carefully spelled out.
4. A supervisor should be permitted to make the maximum number of decisions affecting his employees.
5. Employees should report to only one supervisor.
6. A supervisor should direct only as many employees as he can handle effectively.
7. An organization plan should be flexible.

8. Inspection and performance of work should be separate.
9. Organizational problems should receive immediate attention.
10. Assign work in line with ability and experience.

F. The Four Important Parts of Every Job
1. Inherent in every job is the *accountability* for results.
2. A second set of factors in every job is *responsibilities*.
3. Along with duties and responsibilities one must have the *authority* to act within certain limits without obtaining permission to proceed.
4. No job exists in a vacuum. The supervisor is surrounded by key *relationships*.

G. Principles of Delegation
Where work is delegated for the first time, the supervisor should think in terms of these questions:
1. Who is best qualified to do this?
2. Can an employee improve his abilities by doing this?
3. How long should an employee spend on this?
4. Are there any special problems for which he will need guidance?
5. How broad a delegation can I make?

H. Principles of Effective Communications
1. Determine the media.
2. To whom directed?
3. Identification and source authority.
4. Is communication understood?

I. Principles of Work Improvement
1. Most people usually do only the work which is assigned to them.
2. Workers are likely to fit assigned work into the time available to perform it.
3. A good workload usually stimulates output.
4. People usually do their best work when they know that results will be reviewed or inspected.
5. Employees usually feel that someone else is responsible for conditions of work, workplace layout, job methods, type of tools/equipment, and other such factors.
6. Employees are usually defensive about their job security.
7. Employees have natural resistance to change.
8. Employees can support or destroy a supervisor.
9. A supervisor usually earns the respect of his people through his personal example of diligence and efficiency.

J. Areas of Job Improvement
The areas of job improvement are quite numerous, but the most common ones which a supervisor can identify and utilize are:
1. Departmental layout
2. Flow of work
3. Workplace layout
4. Utilization of manpower
5. Work methods
6. Materials handling

7. Utilization
8. Motion economy

K. Seven Key Points in Making Improvements
1. Select the job to be improved
2. Study how it is being done now
3. Question the present method
4. Determine actions to be taken
5. Chart proposed method
6. Get approval and apply
7. Solicit worker participation

L. Corrective Techniques of Job Improvement
Specific Problems
1. Size of workload
2. Inability to meet schedules
3. Strain and fatigue
4. Improper use of men and skills
5. Waste, poor quality, unsafe conditions
6. Bottleneck conditions that hinder output
7. Poor utilization of equipment and machine
8. Efficiency and productivity of labor

General Improvement
1. Departmental layout
2. Flow of work
3. Work plan layout
4. Utilization of manpower
5. Work methods
6. Materials handling
7. Utilization of equipment
8. Motion economy

Corrective Techniques
1. Study with scale model
2. Flow chart study
3. Motion analysis
4. Comparison of units produced to standard allowance
5. Methods analysis
6. Flow chart and equipment study
7. Down time vs. running time
8. Motion analysis

M. A Planning Checklist
1. Objectives
2. Controls
3. Delegations
4. Communications
5. Resources
6. Manpower

7. Equipment
8. Supplies and materials
9. Utilization of time
10. Safety
11. Money
12. Work
13. Timing of improvements

N. Five Characteristics of Good Directions
In order to get results, directions must be:
1. Possible of accomplishment
2. Agreeable with worker interests
3. Related to mission
4. Planned and complete
5. Unmistakably clear

O. Types of Directions
1. Demands or direct orders
2. Requests
3. Suggestion or implication
4. volunteering

P. Controls
A typical listing of the overall areas in which the supervisor should establish controls might be:
1. Manpower
2. Materials
3. Quality of work
4. Quantity of work
5. Time
6. Space
7. Money
8. Methods

Q. Orienting the New Employee
1. Prepare for him
2. Welcome the new employee
3. Orientation for the job
4. Follow-up

R. Checklist for Orienting New Employees   Yes   No
1. Do you appreciate the feelings of new employees
   when they first report for work?   ___   ___
2. Are you aware of the fact that the new employee must
   make a big adjustment to his job?   ___   ___
3. Have you given him good reasons for liking the job and
   the organization?   ___   ___
4. Have you prepared for his first day on the job?   ___   ___
5. Did you welcome him cordially and make him feel needed?   ___   ___

	Yes	No

6. Did you establish rapport with him so that he feels free to talk and discuss matters with you? ___ ___
7. Did you explain his job to him and his relationship to you? ___ ___
8. Does he know that his work will be evaluated periodically on a basis that is fair and objective? ___ ___
9. Did you introduce him to his fellow workers in such a way that they are likely to accept him? ___ ___
10. Does he know what employee benefits he will receive? ___ ___
11. Does he understand the importance of being on the job and what to do if he must leave his duty station? ___ ___
12. Has he been impressed with the importance of accident prevention and safe practice? ___ ___
13. Does he generally know his way around the department? ___ ___
14. Is he under the guidance of a sponsor who will teach the right way of doing things? ___ ___
15. Do you plan to follow-up so that he will continue to adjust successfully to his job? ___ ___

S. Principles of Learning
   1. Motivation
   2. Demonstration or explanation
   3. Practice

T. Causes of Poor Performance
   1. Improper training for job
   2. Wrong tools
   3. Inadequate directions
   4. Lack of supervisory follow-up
   5. Poor communications
   6. Lack of standards of performance
   7. Wrong work habits
   8. Low morale
   9. Other

U. Four Major Steps in On-The-Job Instruction
   1. Prepare the worker
   2. Present the operation
   3. Tryout performance
   4. Follow-up

V. Employees Want Five Things
   1. Security
   2. Opportunity
   3. Recognition
   4. Inclusion
   5. Expression

W. Some Don'ts in Regard to Praise
    1. Don't praise a person for something he hasn't done.
    2. Don't praise a person unless you can be sincere.
    3. Don't be sparing in praise just because your superior withholds it from you.
    4. Don't let too much time elapse between good performance and recognition of it

X. How to Gain Your Workers' Confidence
    Methods of developing confidence include such things as:
    1. Knowing the interests, habits, hobbies of employees
    2. Admitting your own inadequacies
    3. Sharing and telling of confidence in others
    4. Supporting people when they are in trouble
    5. Delegating matters that can be well handled
    6. Being frank and straightforward about problems and working conditions
    7. Encouraging others to bring their problems to you
    8. Taking action on problems which impede worker progress

Y. Sources of Employee Problems
    On-the-job causes might be such things as:
    1. A feeling that favoritism is exercised in assignments
    2. Assignment of overtime
    3. An undue amount of supervision
    4. Changing methods or systems
    5. Stealing of ideas or trade secrets
    6. Lack of interest in job
    7. Threat of reduction in force
    8. Ignorance or lack of communications
    9. Poor equipment
    10. Lack of knowing how supervisor feels toward employee
    11. Shift assignments

    Off-the-job problems might have to do with:
    1. Health
    2. Finances
    3. Housing
    4. Family

Z. The Supervisor's Key to Discipline
    There are several key points about discipline which the supervisor should keep in mind:
    1. Job discipline is one of the disciplines of life and is directed by the supervisor.
    2. It is more important to correct an employee fault than to fix blame for it.
    3. Employee performance is affected by problems both on the job and off.
    4. Sudden or abrupt changes in behavior can be indications of important employee problems.
    5. Problems should be dealt with as soon as possible after they are identified.
    6. The attitude of the supervisor may have more to do with solving problems than the techniques of problem solving.
    7. Correction of employee behavior should be resorted to only after the supervisor is sure that training or counseling will not be helpful.

8. Be sure to document your disciplinary actions.
9. Make sure that you are disciplining on the basis of facts rather than personal feelings.
10. Take each disciplinary step in order, being careful not to make snap judgments, or decisions based on impatience.

AA. Five Important Processes of Management
1. Planning
2. Organizing
3. Scheduling
4. Controlling
5. Motivating

BB. When the Supervisor Fails to Plan
1. Supervisor creates impression of not knowing his job
2. May lead to excessive overtime
3. Job runs itself—supervisor lacks control
4. Deadlines and appointments missed
5. Parts of the work go undone
6. Work interrupted by emergencies
7. Sets a bad example
8. Uneven workload creates peaks and valleys
9. Too much time on minor details at expense of more important tasks

CC. Fourteen General Principles of Management
1. Division of work
2. Authority and responsibility
3. Discipline
4. Unity of command
5. Unity of direction
6. Subordination of individual interest to general interest
7. Remuneration of personnel
8. Centralization
9. Scalar chain
10. Order
11. Equity
12. Stability of tenure of personnel
13. Initiative
14. Esprit de corps

DD. Change

Bringing about change is perhaps attempted more often, and yet less well understood, than anything else the supervisor does. How do people generally react to change? (People tend to resist change that is imposed upon them by other individuals or circumstances.

Change is characteristic of every situation. It is a part of every real endeavor where the efforts of people are concerned.

1. Why do people resist change?
   People may resist change because of:
   a. Fear of the unknown
   b. Implied criticism
   c. Unpleasant experiences in the past
   d. Fear of loss of status
   e. Threat to the ego
   f. Fear of loss of economic stability

2. How can we best overcome the resistance to change?
   In initiating change, take these steps:
   a. Get ready to sell
   b. Identify sources of help
   c. Anticipate objections
   d. Sell benefits
   e. Listen in depth
   f. Follow up

II. Brief Topical Summaries

   A. Who/What is the Supervisor?
      1. The supervisor is often called the "highest level employee and the lowest level manager."
      2. A supervisor is a member of both management and the work group. He acts as a bridge between the two.
      3. Most problems in supervision are in the area of human relations, or people problems.
      4. Employees expect: Respect, opportunity to learn and to advance, and a sense of belonging, and so forth.
      5. Supervisors are responsible for directing people and organizing work. Planning is of paramount importance.
      6. A position description is a set of duties and responsibilities inherent to a given position.
      7. It is important to keep the position description up-to-date and to provide each employee with his own copy.

   B. The Sociology of Work
      1. People are alike in many ways; however, each individual is unique.
      2. The supervisor is challenged in getting to know employee differences. Acquiring skills in evaluating individuals is an asset.
      3. Maintaining meaningful working relationships in the organization is of great importance.
      4. The supervisor has an obligation to help individuals to develop to their fullest potential.
      5. Job rotation on a planned basis helps to build versatility and to maintain interest and enthusiasm in work groups.
      6. Cross training (job rotation) provides backup skills.

7. The supervisor can help reduce tension by maintaining a sense of humor, providing guidance to employees, and by making reasonable and timely decisions. Employees respond favorably to working under reasonably predictable circumstances.
8. Change is characteristic of all managerial behavior. The supervisor must adjust to changes in procedures, new methods, technological changes, and to a number of new and sometimes challenging situations.
9. To overcome the natural tendency for people to resist change, the supervisor should become more skillful in initiating change.

C. Principles and Practices of Supervision
1. Employees should be required to answer to only one superior.
2. A supervisor can effectively direct only a limited number of employees, depending upon the complexity, variety, and proximity of the jobs involved.
3. The organizational chart presents the organization in graphic form. It reflects lines of authority and responsibility as well as interrelationships of units within the organization.
4. Distribution of work can be improved through an analysis using the "Work Distribution Chart."
5. The "Work Distribution Chart" reflects the division of work within a unit in understandable form.
6. When related tasks are given to an employee, he has a better chance of increasing his skills through training.
7. The individual who is given the responsibility for tasks must also be given the appropriate authority to insure adequate results.
8. The supervisor should delegate repetitive, routine work. Preparation of recurring reports, maintaining leave and attendance records are some examples.
9. Good discipline is essential to good task performance. Discipline is reflected in the actions of employees on the job in the absence of supervision.
10. Disciplinary action may have to be taken when the positive aspects of discipline have failed. Reprimand, warning, and suspension are examples of disciplinary action.
11. If a situation calls for a reprimand, be sure it is deserved and remember it is to be done in private.

D. Dynamic Leadership
1. A style is a personal method or manner of exerting influence.
2. Authoritarian leaders often see themselves as the source of power and authority.
3. The democratic leader often perceives the group as the source of authority and power.
4. Supervisors tend to do better when using the pattern of leadership that is most natural for them.
5. Social scientists suggest that the effective supervisor use the leadership style that best fits the problem or circumstances involved.
6. All four styles—telling, selling, consulting, joining—have their place. Using one does not preclude using the other at another time.

7. The theory X point of view assumes that the average person dislikes work, will avoid it whenever possible, and must be coerced to achieve organizational objectives.
8. The theory Y point of view assumes that the average person considers work to be a natural as play, and, when the individual is committed, he requires little supervision or direction to accomplish desired objectives.
9. The leader's basic assumptions concerning human behavior and human nature affect his actions, decisions, and other managerial practices.
10. Dissatisfaction among employees is often present, but difficult to isolate. The supervisor should seek to weaken dissatisfaction by keeping promises, being sincere and considerate, keeping employees informed, and so forth.
11. Constructive suggestions should be encouraged during the natural progress of the work.

E. Processes for Solving Problems
   1. People find their daily tasks more meaningful and satisfying when they can improve them.
   2. The causes of problems, or the key factors, are often hidden in the background. Ability to solve problems often involves the ability to isolate them from their backgrounds. There is some substance to the cliché that some persons "can't see the forest for the trees."
   3. New procedures are often developed from old ones. Problems should be broken down into manageable parts. New ideas can be adapted from old one.
   4. People think differently in problem-solving situations. Using a logical, patterned approach is often useful. One approach found to be useful includes these steps:
      a. Define the problem
      b. Establish objectives
      c. Get the facts
      d. Weigh and decide
      e. Take action
      f. Evaluate action

F. Training for Results
   1. Participants respond best when they feel training is important to them.
   2. The supervisor has responsibility for the training and development of those who report to him.
   3. When training is delegated to others, great care must be exercised to insure the trainer has knowledge, aptitude, and interest for his work as a trainer.
   4. Training (learning) of some type goes on continually. The most successful supervisor makes certain the learning contributes in a productive manner to operational goals.
   5. New employees are particularly susceptible to training. Older employees facing new job situations require specific training, as well as having need for development and growth opportunities.
   6. Training needs require continuous monitoring.
   7. The training officer of an agency is a professional with a responsibility to assist supervisors in solving training problems.

8. Many of the self-development steps important to the supervisor's own growth are equally important to the development of peers and subordinates. Knowledge of these is important when the supervisor consults with others on development and growth opportunities.

G. Health, Safety, and Accident Prevention
1. Management-minded supervisors take appropriate measures to assist employees in maintaining health and in assuring safe practices in the work environment.
2. Effective safety training and practices help to avoid injury and accidents.
3. Safety should be a management goal. All infractions of safety which are observed should be corrected without exception.
4. Employees' safety attitude, training and instruction, provision of safe tools and equipment, supervision, and leadership are considered highly important factors which contribute to safety and which can be influenced directly by supervisors.
5. When accidents do occur, they should be investigated promptly for very important reasons, including the fact that information which is gained can be used to prevent accidents in the future.

H. Equal Employment Opportunity
1. The supervisor should endeavor to treat all employees fairly, without regard to religion, race, sex, or national origin.
2. Groups tend to reflect the attitude of the leader. Prejudice can be detected even in very subtle form. Supervisors must strive to create a feeling of mutual respect and confidence in every employee.
3. Complete utilization of all human resources is a national goal. Equitable consideration should be accorded women in the work force, minority-group members, the physically and mentally handicapped, and the older employee. The important question is: "Who can do the job?"
4. Training opportunities, recognition for performance, overtime assignments, promotional opportunities, and all other personnel actions are to be handled on an equitable basis.

I. Improving Communications
1. Communications is achieving understanding between the sender and the receiver of a message. It also means sharing information—the creation of understanding.
2. Communication is basic to all human activity. Words are means of conveying meanings; however, real meanings are in people.
3. There are very practical differences in the effectiveness of one-way, impersonal, and two-way communications. Words spoken face-to-face are better understood. Telephone conversations are effective, but lack the rapport of person-to-person exchanges. The whole person communicates.
4. Cooperation and communication in an organization go hand in hand. When there is a mutual respect between people, spelling out rules and procedures for communicating is unnecessary.
5. There are several barriers to effective communications. These include failure to listen with respect and understanding, lack of skill in feedback, and misinterpreting the meanings of words used by the speaker. It is also common

practice to listen to what we want to hear, and tune out things we do not want to hear.
6. Communication is management's chief problem. The supervisor should accept the challenge to communicate more effectively and to improve interagency and intra-agency communications.
7. The supervisor may often plan for and conduct meetings. The planning phase is critical and may determine the success or the failure of a meeting.
8. Speaking before groups usually requires extra effort. Stage fright may never disappear completely, but it can be controlled.

J. Self-Development
1. Every employee is responsible for his own self-development.
2. Toastmaster and toastmistress clubs offer opportunities to improve skills in oral communications.
3. Planning for one's own self-development is of vital importance. Supervisors know their own strengths and limitations better than anyone else.
4. Many opportunities are open to aid the supervisor in his developmental efforts, including job assignments; training opportunities, both governmental and non-governmental—to include universities and professional conferences and seminars.
5. Programmed instruction offers a means of studying at one's own rate.
6. Where difficulties may arise from a supervisor's being away from his work for training, he may participate in televised home study or correspondence courses to meet his self-development needs.

K. Teaching and Training
1. The Teaching Process
Teaching is encouraging and guiding the learning activities of students toward established goals. In most cases this process consists of five steps: preparation, presentation, summarization, evaluation, and application.

   a. Preparation
   Preparation is two-fold in nature; that of the supervisor and the employee. Preparation by the supervisor is absolutely essential to success. He must know what, when, where, how, and whom he will teach. Some of the factors that should be considered are:
   1) The objectives
   2) The materials needed
   3) The methods to be used
   4) Employee participation
   5) Employee interest
   6) Training aids
   7) Evaluation
   8) Summarization

   Employee preparation consists in preparing the employee to receive the material. Probably the most important single factor in the preparation of the employee is arousing and maintaining his interest. He must know the objectives of the training, why he is there, how the material can be used, and its importance to him.

b. Presentation
In presentation, have a carefully designed plan and follow it. The plan should be accurate and complete, yet flexible enough to meet situations as they arise. The method of presentation will be determined by the particular situation and objectives.

c. Summary
A summary should be made at the end of every training unit and program. In addition, there may be internal summaries depending on the nature of the material being taught. The important thing is that the trainee must always be able to understand how each part of the new material relates to the whole.

d. Application
The supervisor must arrange work so the employee will be given a chance to apply new knowledge or skills while the material is still clear in his mind and interest is high. The trainee does not really know whether he has learned the material until he has been given a chance to apply it. If the material is not applied, it loses most of its value.

e. Evaluation
The purpose of all training is to promote learning. To determine whether the training has been a success or failure, the supervisor must evaluate this learning.
In the broadest sense, evaluation includes all the devices, methods, skills, and techniques used by the supervisor to keep himself and the employees informed as to their progress toward the objectives they are pursuing. The extent to which the employee has mastered the knowledge, skills, and abilities, or changed his attitudes, as determined by the program objectives, is the extent to which instruction has succeeded or failed.
Evaluation should not be confined to the end of the lesson, day, or program but should be used continuously. We shall note later the way this relates to the rest of the teaching process.

2. Teaching Methods
A teaching method is a pattern of identifiable student and instructor activity used in presenting training material.
All supervisors are faced with the problem of deciding which method should be used at a given time.

a. Lecture
The lecture is direct oral presentation of material by the supervisor. The present trend is to place less emphasis on the trainer's activity and more on that of the trainee.

b. Discussion
Teaching by discussion or conference involves using questions and other techniques to arouse interest and focus attention upon certain areas, and by doing so creating a learning situation. This can be one of the most

valuable methods because it gives the employees an opportunity to express their ideas and pool their knowledge.

c. Demonstration
The demonstration is used to teach how something works or how to do something. It can be used to show a principle or what the results of a series of actions will be. A well-staged demonstration is particularly effective because it shows proper methods of performance in a realistic manner.

d. Performance
Performance is one of the most fundamental of all learning techniques or teaching methods. The trainee may be able to tell how a specific operation should be performed but he cannot be sure he knows how to perform the operation until he has done so.
As with all methods, there are certain advantages and disadvantages to each method.

e. Which Method to Use
Moreover, there are other methods and techniques of teaching. It is difficult to use any method without other methods entering into it. In any learning situation, a combination of methods is usually more effective than any one method alone.

Finally, evaluation must be integrated into the other aspects of the teaching-learning process.

It must be used in the motivation of the trainees; it must be used to assist in developing understanding during the training; and it must be related to employee application of the results of training.

This is distinctly the role of the supervisor.